THE RISE OF THE DUTCH KINGDOM

1795-1813

A SHORT ACCOUNT OF THE
EARLY DEVELOPMENT OF THE MODERN
KINGDOM OF THE NETHERLANDS

By

HENDRIK WILLEM VAN LOON

First published in 1915

This edition published by Read Books Ltd.
Copyright © 2019 Read Books Ltd.
This book is copyright and may not be
reproduced or copied in any way without
the express permission of the publisher in writing

British Library Cataloguing-in-Publication Data
A catalogue record for this book is available
from the British Library

DEDICATION

This little book, telling the story of our national usurpation by a foreign enemy during the beginning of the nineteenth century, appears at a moment when our nearest neighbours are suffering the same fate which befell us more than a hundred years ago.

I dedicate my work to the five soldiers of the Belgian army who saved my life near Waerloos.

I hope that their grandchildren may read a story of national revival which will be as complete and happy as that of our own land.

Brussels, Belgium,
Christmas night, 1914.

CONTENTS

APOLOGIA 9

FOREWORD 10

DRAMATIS PERSONÆ. 13

PROLOGUE 18

I THE LAST DAYS OF THE OLD ORDER 22

II THE REVOLUTION. 36

III THE COST OF REVOLUTION 46

IV THE PROVISIONAL. 52

V SOLEMN OPENING OF THE
NATIONAL ASSEMBLY 61

THE OPENING CEREMONIES 61

VI PIETER PAULUS 66

VII NATIONAL ASSEMBLY NO. I AT WORK. 70

VIII NATIONAL ASSEMBLY NO. II AT WORK 76

IX GLORY ABROAD 82

X COUP D'ÉTAT NO. I 86

XI THE CONSTITUTIONAL. 93

XII COUP D'ÉTAT NO. II. 97

XIII CONSTITUTION NO. II AT WORK 103

XIV MORE GLORY ABROAD 105

XV CONSTITUTION NO. III 111

XVI THE THIRD CONSTITUTION AT WORK 115

XVII ECONOMIC CONDITION. 117

XVIII SOCIAL LIFE. 124

XIX PEACE. 130

XX SCHIMMELPENNINCK 135

XXI KING LOUIS OF HOLLAND 142

XXII THE DEPARTMENT FORMERLY
CALLED HOLLAND. 149

XXIII LIBERATION. 158

XXIV THE RESTORATION. 168

XXV WILLIAM I 172

A COMPARISON OF THE FOUR
CONSTITUTIONS OF HOLLAND. 181

BIBLIOGRAPHY GIVING THE DETAILS
OF THE RESURRECTION OF
HOLLAND IN 1812 186

THE BATAVIAN REPUBLIC. 187

THE KINGDOM OF HOLLAND 192

FRENCH OCCUPATION 194

THE RESTORATION. 195

ILLUSTRATIONS

William I 8

1795. Dutch Republic—Reproduced from Author's Sketch 26

The Estates of Holland 29

Flight of William V 31

line map 33

Krayenhoff 35

Warship Entering the Port of Amsterdam 39

Daendels 42

French troops entering Amsterdam 43

Capetown captured by the English 56

Pieter Paulus 65

The National Assembly 69

The speaker of the Assembly welcoming the
French Minister 73

1797 Batavian Republic 77

De landing der Engelschen. Invasion of the British 107

Dutch troops rushing to the defence of the coast 109

Armed bark of the year 1801 116

The Executive Council of the East India Company 118

Dutch ships frozen in the ice 120

Batavia—The fashionable quarter 123

A country place 123

Skating on the river Maas at Rotterdam 125

Trades 127

Schimmelpenninck 134

Schimmelpenninck arrives at The Hague 138

Louis Napoleon 141

1807. Kingdom of Holland. 145

Napoleon visits Amsterdam 148

1811. Holland annexed by France. 150

Reproduced from Author's Sketch.. 151

Departure of Gardes d'Honneur from Amsterdam 154

Gysbert Karel Van Hogendorp 157

Proclamation of the new Government. 162

Arrival of William I in Scheveningen 167

Kingdom of the Netherlands. 173

Lieutenant Van Speyck blows up his ship 175

King William II 177

William I

APOLOGIA

And for those other faults of barbarism, Doric dialect, extemporanean style, tautologies, apish imitation, a rhapsody of rags gathered together from several dung-hills, excrements of authors, toys and fopperies confusedly tumbled out, without art, invention, judgment, wit, learning, harsh, raw, rude, fantastical, absurd, insolent, indiscreet, ill-composed, indigested, vain, scurrile, idle, dull, and dry, I confess all ('tis partly affected); thou canst not think worse of me than I do of myself.

So that as a river runs, sometimes precipitate and swift, then dull and slow; now direct, then *per ambages*; now deep, then shallow; now muddy, then clear; now broad, then narrow; doth my style flow: now serious, then light; now comical, then satirical; now more elaborate, then remiss, as the present subject required or as at that time I was affected. And if thou vouchsafe to read this treatise, it shall seem no otherwise to thee than the way to an ordinary traveller, sometimes fair, sometimes foul, here champaign, there enclosed; barren in one place, better soil in another.

—*Anatomy of Melancholy.*
—Burton.

FOREWORD

This foreword is an afterthought. It was written when the first proofs of the book had gone back to the printer. And this is how it took its origin:

A few days ago I received a copy of a Dutch historical magazine containing a violent attack upon one of my former books. The reviewer, who evidently neither had taken the time to read my book nor had taken the trouble to understand what I was trying to say, accused me among other things of a haughty contempt for my forefathers during their time of decline. Haughty contempt, indeed! Nay, Brother of the Acrid Pen, was it not the truth which hurt thee so unexpectedly rather than my scornful irony?

There are those who claim that reviews do not matter. There are those who, when their work is talked about with supercilious ignorance, claim that an author ought to forget what has been said about his work. Pious wish! The writer who really cares for his work can no more forget an undeserved insult to the product of his brain than he can forgive a harsh word given unmerited to one of his children. The thing rankles. And in my desire to see a pleasant face, to talk this hurt away, as soon as I arrived this morning in New York I went to see a friend. He has an office downtown. It overlooks the harbour. From its window one beholds the Old World entering the new one by way of the Ellis Island ferryboat.

It was early and I had to wait. Over the water there hung a low, thin mist. Sea-gulls, very white against the gray sky, were circling about. And then suddenly, in the distance, there appeared a dark form coming sliding slowly through the fog. And through a window, opened to get over the suffocating effect of the steam-heat, there sounded the vibrating tones of a hoarse steam-whistle—a sound which brought back to me my earliest years spent among ships and craft of all sorts, and queer noises of water and wind and steam. And then, after a minute, I recognized by its green and white funnel that it was one of our own ships which was coming up the harbour.

And at that instant everything upon which I had been brooding became so clear to me that I took to the nearest typewriter, and there, in front of that same open window, I sit and write what I have understood but a moment ago.

Once, we have been a very great people. We have had a slow decline and we have had a fall which we caused by our own mistakes and during which we showed the worst sides of our character. But now all this has changed. And at the present moment we have a better claim to a place on the honour-list of nations than the mere fact that once upon a time, some three centuries ago, our ancestors did valiant deeds.

For, more important, because more difficult of accomplishment, there stands this one supreme fact: we have come back.

What I shall have to tell you in the following pages, if you are inclined to regard it as such, will read like a mockery of one's own people.

But who is there that has studied the events of those years between 1795-1815 who did not feel the utter indignation, the terrible shame, of so much cowardice, of such hopeless vacillation in the hour of need, of such indifference to civic duties? Who has ever tried to understand the events of the year of Restoration who does not know that there was very little glory connected with an event which the self-contented contemporary delighted to compare to the great days of the struggle against Spanish tyranny? And who that has studied the history of the early nineteenth century does not know how for two whole generations after the Napoleonic wars our country was no better than a negative power, tolerated because so inoffensive? And who, when he compares what was one hundred years ago with what is to-day, can fail to see what a miracle of human energy here has happened? I have no statistics at hand to tell you about our shipping, our imports and exports, or to show you the very favourable place which the next to the smallest among the nations occupies. Nor can I, without looking it up, write down for your benefit what we have invented, have written, have painted. Nor is it my desire to show you in detail how the old neglected inheritance of the East India Company has been transformed into a colonial empire where not only the intruding Hollander but where the native, too, has a free chance to develop and to prosper.

But what I can say and will say with all emphasis is this: Look where you will, in whatever quarter of the globe you desire, and you will find Holland again upholding her old traditions for efficiency, energy, and tenacity of purpose.

Pay a visit to the Hollander at home and you will find that he is trying to solve with the same ancient industry of research the eternal problems of nature, while with the utmost spirit of modern times he attempts to reconstruct the relationship between those who have and those who have not, until a basis mutually more beneficial shall have been established. Then you will see how upon all sides there has been a return to a renewed interest in life and to a desire to do cheerfully those tasks which the country has been set to do.

And then you will understand how the year 1913, proud of what has been achieved, though not content that the goal has been reached, can well afford to tell the truth about the year 1813. For after a century and a half of decline Holland once more has aspired to be great in everything in which a small nation can be great.

New York, N.Y., October 31, 1913.

DRAMATIS PERSONÆ

DRAMATIS PERSONÆ (*in order of their appearance*).

CURTAIN: *December, 1795.*

William V: Last hereditary Stadholder, futile, well-meaning, but without any conception of the events which during the latter half of the eighteenth century brought about the new order of things. Unable to institute the highly necessary centralization of the country and emancipate the middle classes, which for the last three centuries have been cut totally out of all political power. He is driven out by the French Revolution more than by his own discontented countrymen. Dies, forgotten, on his country estates in Germany.

The Patriots: Mildly revolutionary party, since the middle of the eighteenth century working for a more centralized and somewhat more representative government. Belong almost without exception to the professional and higher middle classes. Represented in the new Batavian Assemblies mostly under the name of Unionists.

The Regents: The old plutocratic oligarchy. Disappear with the triumph of the Patriots. Continue opposition to the centralizing process, but for all intents and purposes they have played their little rôle when the old republic ceases to be.

The Federalists: Combine all the opposition elements in

the new Batavian Republic which work to maintain the old decentralization.

Daendels: Lawyer, cart-tail orator, professional exile. Fallen hero of the Patriotic struggles; flees to Belgium when the Prussians in 1787 restore William V to his old dignities. Returns in 1795 as quite a hero and a French major-general. Later with French help organizes a number of *coups d'état* which finally remove the opposing Federalists and give the power to the Unionists. A capable man in many ways. An enthusiast who spared others as little as he did himself.

Krayenhoff: Doctor, physicist, experiments in new medical theories with same cheer he does in the new science of politics. Able and efficient in everything he undertakes. Too much of a man of principle and honesty to make much of a career during revolutionary days.

Pieter Paulus: The sort of man who twenty years before might have saved the Republic if only the Stadholder had known how to avail himself of such a simple citizen possessed of so much common sense. Trained thoroughly in the intricate working of the Republic's government. Scrupulously honest. So evidently the One and Only Man to lead the new Batavian Republic that he was killed immediately by overwork.

Schimmelpenninck: Lawyer, man of unselfish patriotism, honest, careful, no sense of humour, but a very sober sense of the practically possible. No lover of extremes, but in no way blind to the impossibility of maintaining the old, outworn system of government. Tries at his own private inconvenience to save the country, but when he fails keeps the everlasting respect of both his enemies and those who were supposed to be his friends.

France, or, rather, the French Revolution, regards the Republic in the same way in which a poor man looks upon a rich man with a beefsteak. Being possessed of a strong club, it hits the rich man on the head, grabs his steak, his clothes, everything he possesses, and then makes him turn about and fight his former friends.

Liberty, Equality, and Fraternity: Trademark patented by the French Republic between the years 1790 and 1809. The goods covered by this trademark soon greatly deteriorate and finally cover a rank imitation of the original article.

Napoleon Bonaparte: Chief salesman of the above article for the territory abroad. Further references unnecessary. Gets a controlling hold of the firm in which at first he was a subordinate. Removes the article which made him successful from the market and introduces a new brand, covered merely with a big N. Firm fails in 1815. The involuntary customers pay the deficit.

England: Chief enemy of above. In self-defence against the Franco-Dutch combination, it takes all of the Republic's outlying territories.

Louis Napoleon: Second brother of Napoleon Bonaparte. Only gentleman of the family. Made King of Holland in anticipation of a complete French annexation. Makes an honest but useless attempt to prevent this annexation. Wife (Napoleon's stepdaughter) no good. Son, Napoleon III, Emperor of the French.

Le Brun, Duke of Plaisance: Governor of the annexed Republic. Makes the very best of a rather odious job. Far superior to the corps of brigands who were his subordinates.

Van Hogendorp: Incarnation of the better elements of the old order; supporter of William V, although very much aware of the uselessness of that prince. Has seen a little more of the world than most of his contemporaries. During the Batavian

Republic and annexation refuses to have anything to do with what he considers an illegitimate form of government. Man of great strength who, practically alone, arranges the Revolution of 1813, which drives out the French before the European allies can conquer the Republic.

William I: First constitutional King of Holland, oldest son of William V, has learned a good deal abroad, but only during the last ten years of his exile. Personally a man of the Old Régime, but with too excellent a business sense not to see that the times have changed. Rather too much a business man and too little a statesman. Excellent organizer. In many ways too energetic. Pity he did not live a hundred years later.

Of the real people we shall see very little. A small minority, very small indeed, will try to make a noise like Jacobins. But their little comedy is abruptly ended by the great French stage manager every time he thinks that such rowdy acting is no longer suitable. Unfortunately for themselves, they began their particular acting three years later than Paris, and, fortunately for the rest of us, the sort of plays written around the guillotine were no longer popular in France when the managers in Holland wished to introduce them. The majority of the people, however, gradually impoverished by eternal taxation, without the old revenues from the colonies, with their sons enlisted and serving a bad cause in foreign armies—the majority takes to a disastrous way of vegetating at home, takes to leading an introspective and non-constructive religious life, finally despairing of everything save paternal despotism.

In the country everything becomes Frenchified. The fashions are the fashions of Paris (two years late). Furniture, books, literature, everything except an old-fashioned and narrow orthodoxy becomes a true but clumsy copy of the French.

The other actors in our little play are foreigners: Sansculottes, French soldiers of all arms, British and Russian invaders, captives from all of the Lord's countries, French customs officers, French policemen, French spies, adventurers of every sort and nationality; French bands playing the "Carmagnole" and "Marseillaise," *ad infinitum* and *ad nauseam*.

Finally Cossacks, Russian Infantry, Blücher Hussars, followed by a sudden and wild crowd of citizens waving orange colours. And then, once more for many years, dull, pious citizens, taking no interest in anything but their own respectability, looking at the world from behind closed curtains, so terribly hit by adversity that they no longer dare to be active. Until this generation gradually takes the road to the welcome cemetery, the curtains are pulled up, the windows are opened, and a fresh spirit of energy and enterprise is allowed to blow through the old edifice, and the old fear of living is replaced by the desire to take an active part in the work of the greater world.

PROLOGUE

And now—behold the scene changes.

The old Republic of the United Netherlands, once the stronghold of an incipient liberty, the asylum to which for many centuries fled all those who were persecuted—this same republic will be regarded by the disciples of the great French Revolution as another Bastille of usurped power, as the incarnation of all despotic principles, and will soon be demolished by its own eager citizens. The ruins will be carted away as so much waste material, unworthy of being used in the great New Temple now to be constructed to the truly divine principles of Liberty, Fraternity, and Equality. The old Stadholder, last representative of the illustrious House of Orange, alternately the Father of his Country and the Beast of the Book of Revelation, will flee for his life and will spend the rest of his days in England or Germany, nobody knows and nobody cares where. Their High and Mightinesses of the Estates, proud little potentates once accustomed to full sovereign honours, refusing to receive the most important communication unless provided with their full and correct titles, these same High and Mightinesses will have to content themselves with the even greater honour of being called Citizen Representatives. Their ancient meeting hall, too sacred to allow the keeping of official records of their meetings, will be the sight of the town and will be patronized by the loafers to whom the rights of men mean a Maypole, the tricolor, free gin, and a brass band. Why go on with a minute recital? The end of the world has come. The days of tyranny, of indignity to the sovereign sanctity of the individual, are over. Regents, coal-heavers, patriots, fish peddlers, officers and soldiers, soon they are all to be of the same human clay. The vote of one is as good as that of the other. Wherefore, in the name of Equality, give them all a chance and see what will come of it. If a constitution does not suit at the first attempt, use it to feed a patriotic bonfire. After all, what else is it but some woodpulp and printer's ink? If the parliament of to-day does not please the voters of to-morrow, dissolve it, close it with the help of gendarmes. If the members resist, call out the reserves or borrow some soldiers from the great sister republic, which is now teaching her blessed creed to all the world. They (the soldiers) are there for the asking (and for the paying). They are a little out at the elbows, very much out in regard to shoes, and they have not seen a real piece of money for many a weary month, but for a square meal and a handful of paper greenbacks they will dismiss a parliament, rob a museum, or levy taxes, with the utmost fidelity to their orders and with strict discipline to their master's commands.

Then, if constitutions and parliaments have failed in an equal degree, humbly beg for a king from among that remarkable family the father of which was a little pettifogging lawyer in a third-rate Italian city, and the members of which now rule one half of the European continent.

After the rights of men, the rights of a single man.

In the great melting pot of the Bonapartistic empire all Hollanders at last become equal in the real sense of the word. They all have the same chance at promotion, at riches, and the pursuit of happiness. Devotion to the master, and devotion to him alone, will bring recognition from the new divinity who issues orders signed with a single gigantic N. Old Republic of the United Netherlands, enlightened Republic of the Free Batavian Proconsulate, Kingdom of Holland, it's all the same to the man who regards this little land as so much mud, deposited by his own, his French, rivers.

Vainly and desperately the bankrupt little Kingdom of Brother Louis has struggled to maintain a semblance of independence.

A piece of paper, a big splotchy N, and the whole comedy is over.

The High and Mightinesses, the Citizen Representatives, First

Consul, Royal Majesty, all the big and little political wirepullers of fifteen years of unstable government, are swept away, are told to hold their peace, and to contribute money and men, money and men, more money and men, to carry the glory of the capital N to the uttermost corners of the world. Never mind about their government, their language, the remembrance of the old days of glorious renown. The old days are over for good. The language has no right to exist save as a patois for rustic yokels. As for the government, gold-laced adventurers, former barkeepers, and prize-fighters, now bearers of historic titles, will be sent to look after that. They come with an army of followers, tax-gatherers, policemen, and spies. They execute their duties in the most approved Napoleonic fashion. There is war in Spain and there is war in Russia. There is murder to be done in Portugal, and there is plunder to be gathered in Germany. The Hollander does not care for this sort of work. Never mind his private likes and dislikes! Hang a few, shoot a few, and the rest will march fast enough! And so, up and down the Spanish peninsula, up but not down the Russian steppes, the Hollander who cared too much for trade to bother about politics is forced to march for the glory of that letter N. Amsterdam is reduced from the richest city in Europe to a forgotten nest, where the grass grows on the streets and where half of the population is kept alive by public charity. What matters it? His Majesty has reviewed the new Polish and Lithuanian regiments and is highly contented with their appearance. The British have taken all the colonies, and the people eat grass for bread and drink chiccory for coffee. Who cares? His Majesty has bought a new goat cart for the King of Rome, his august son, and is tremendously pleased with the new acquisition. The country is bankrupt. Such a simple matter! Some more paper, another scrawly N, and the State debt is reduced by two thirds. A hundred thousand families are ruined, but his Majesty sleeps as well as ever and indeed never felt better in his life. Until this capital letter goes the way of all big and small letters of the historical alphabet, and is put away in Clio's box of enormities for all time—

And then, O patient reader, who wonders what all this rhetoric is leading to, what shall we then have to tell you?

How out of the ruin of untried schemes, the terrible failures, the heartbreaking miseries of these two decades of honest enthusiasm and dishonest exploitation, there arose a new State, built upon a firmer ground than ever before, ready and willing to take upon itself the burden and the duties of a modern community, and showing in the next century that nothing is lost as long as the spirit of hopefulness and cheerful work and the firm belief in one's own destiny are allowed to survive material ruin. Amen.

I.

THE LAST DAYS OF THE OLD ORDER

DECEMBER, 1795

It is the year of grace 1795, and the eighth of the glorious French Revolution. For almost a century there has been friction between the different parts of the population. A new generation has grown up in an atmosphere of endless political debate—finally of mere political scandal. But now the days of idle discussions are over. More than forty years before, manifestly in the year 1745, the intelligent middle classes began their agitation for a share in the government, a government which during the days of great commercial prosperity has fallen entirely into the hands of the capitalistic classes. In this struggle, reasonable enough in itself, they have looked for guidance to the House of Orange.

Alas! those princes who so often have led the people, who have made this nation what it is, whose name has come to stand for the very land of which they are the hired executives—these princes now no longer are in direct touch with the basic part of the nation. This time they have failed to see their manifest duty. Left to their own devices, the reformers, the Patriots as they are commonly called, have fallen into bad hands. They have mistaken mere rhetoric for action. They have allowed themselves to be advised by hot-headed young men, raw boys, filled with undigested philosophies borrowed from their better-instructed neighbours. As their allies they have taken experienced politicians who were willing to use this party of enthusiasts for their own selfish purposes. More through the mistakes of their enemies than through the virtue of their own partisans, the Patriots have gained a victory in the Chambers of the old Estates, where the clumsy machinery of the republican government, outworn and ill-fitted for modern demands, rolls on like some forgotten water-wheel in an ancient forest.

This victory, however, has been won too easily to be of any value to the conqueror. The Patriots, believing themselves safe behind their wall of mere words, have gone out of their way to insult the hereditary Stadholder. What is worse, they have given offence to his wife, the sister of the King of Prussia. Ten years before, in the last English war, through a policy of criminal ignorance, they risked their country's last bit of naval strength in an uneven quarrel. This time (we mean the year 1787) they bring upon themselves the military strength of the best-drilled country of the western world. In less than one week the Prussians have blown together this card-house of the Dutch Patriots. Their few untrained soldiers have fled without firing a single shot. Stadholder William once more drives in state to his ancestral palace in the woods, and again his clumsy fingers try to unravel the perplexing maze of this antiquated government—with the same result as before. He cannot do it. Truth is, that the old government is hopelessly beyond repair. Demolition and complete reconstruction alone will save the country from anarchy. But where is the man with the courage and the tenacity of purpose to undertake this gigantic task? Certainly it is not William, to whom a new cockade on the cap of his soldiers is of vastly more importance than a reform of the legislative power. Nor can anything be hoped from old Van den Spiegel, the Raadpensionaris, a man nearing the seventies, who desires more the rest of his comfortable Zeeland estate than the hopeless management of an impossible government. There is, of course, the Princess Wilhelmina, the wife of William, a woman possessed of all the strength and executive ability of her great-uncle Frederick, the late King of Prussia. But just now she is regarded as the arch-traitress, the Jezebel of the country. Alone she can do nothing, and among the gold-laced brethren who doze in the princely anterooms there is not a man of even mediocre ability.

For a short while a young man, trained abroad, capable observer, shrewd in the judgment of his fellow-men, and willing to make personal sacrifices for his principles, has supported her with vigorous counsel. But he, too, has given up the hopeless task of inciting the Stadholder to deeds of energy, and we shall not hear the name of Gysbrecht Karel van Hogendorp until twenty years later, when in the quiet of his study he shall prepare the first draft of the constitution of the new Kingdom of the Netherlands and shall make ready for the revolution which must overthrow the French yoke.

In Rotterdam, leading the uneventful life of a civilian director of the almost defunct Admiralty, there is Pieter Paulus, who for a moment promised to play the rôle of a Dutch Mirabeau. He, too, however, found no elements with which he could do any constructive work. He has retired to his books and vouchers, trying to solve the puzzle of how to pay captains and sailors out of an empty treasury.

A country of a million and a half of people, a country which for more than a century has led the destinies of Europe, cannot be devoid of capable men in so short a time? Then—where are they? Most of them are still within the boundaries of the old republic. But disheartened by the disgrace of foreign invasion, by the muddling of Patriot and regent, they sulk at home and await the things that are bound to come. Many citizens, some say 40,000, but probably less than 30,000, have fled the country and are exiled abroad. They fill the little Belgian cities along the Dutch frontier. They live from hand to mouth. They petition the government in Paris, they solicit help from the government in London, they will appeal to everybody who may have anything to give, be he friend or enemy. When support is not forthcoming— and usually the petitioned party turns a deaf ear—they run up a bill at the little political club where their credit is good, until the steward himself shall go into bankruptcy. Then they renew their old appeals, until finally they receive a few grudging guilders, and as barroom politicians they await the day of vengeance and a return to the fraternal fleshpots.

Meanwhile in The Hague, where, as of old, the Stadholder plays at being a little monarch, what is being done? Nothing!

The year 1789 comes and brings the beginning of the great French Revolution. The government of the republic thinks of the frightful things that might have happened if the Patriots, instead of the Prussians, had been successful in 1787, and it draws the lines of reaction tighter than before. At the same time a new business depression sets in. Large banking houses fail. The West India Company of glorious memory is dissolved and put into the receiver's hands.

Two years more and France declares war upon the republic and upon England. The unwilling people are urged to fight, but refuse. Town after town is surrendered without the firing of a single shot. It was the dissension in the French camp—it was the treason of Dumouriez—which this time saved the country, not the bravery of its soldiers. And the moment the French had reorganized their forces, the cause of the Stadholder was lost. In the years 1794 and 1795 new attacks followed. Driven into a corner, with a vague feeling that this time it meant the end of things, the defence showed a little more courage than before. Of organization, however, there was not a vestige. In between useless fortifications, insufficiently manned and badly defended, the French Revolutionary armies walked straight to the well-filled coffers of rich Amsterdam.

It was midwinter. The rivers were frozen. How often had the ice served the invader as a welcome road into this impassable country! And just how often had not divine Providence interfered with a timely thaw and had changed the victorious inroad into a disastrous rout? It had happened time and again during the rebellion against Spain. It had happened in the year 1672 when the cowardly neglect of a Dutch commander alone had saved the army of Louis XIV from total annihilation.

Again, in this year of grace 1795, the people expected a miracle. But miracles do not come to those who are not prepared to help themselves. The frost continued. For two weeks the thermometer did not rise above the freezing point. The Maas and the Waal, large rivers which were seldom frozen over, became solid banks of ice. Wherever the French troops crossed them they were welcomed as deliverers. The country, honeycombed with treason, overrun with hungry exiles hastening home to a bed with clean linen, and a well-filled pantry, hailed the ragged sansculottes as the bringers of a new day of light.

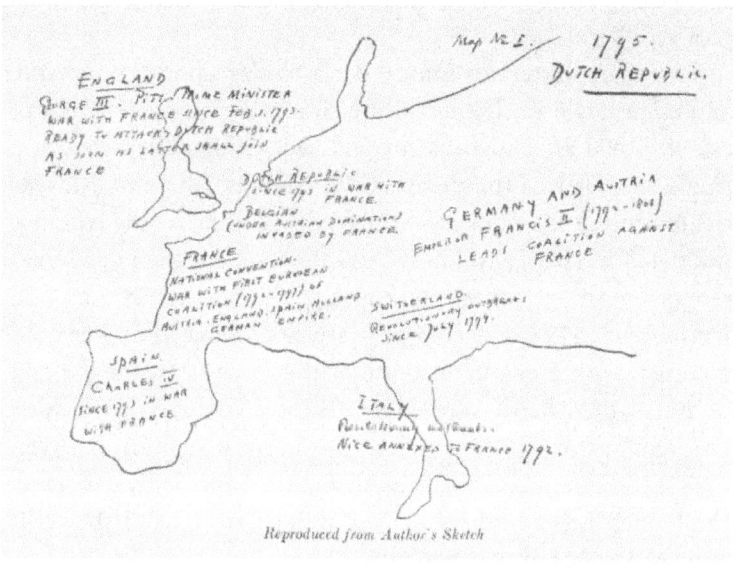

1795. Dutch Republic—Reproduced from Author's Sketch

William, among his turnip-gardens and his little bodyguard, surrounded by his trivial court, wondered what the end was going to be. When first he entered upon the struggle with the Patriots it was the head of old King Charles which had haunted him in his dreams. Now he had fresh visions of another but similar episode. Two years before his good brother, the Citizen Capet, had climbed the scaffold for his last view of his rebellious subjects. Since then all that was highest and finest and noblest in the French capital had trundled down the road which led to the Place de la Concorde.

William was not of the stock of which heroes and martyrs are made. What was to become of him when the French should reach The Hague? The advance guard of the invading army was now in Utrecht. One day's distance for good cavalry separated the revolutionary soldiers from the Dutch capital.

The jewels and other valuables of the princely family had been sent away three months before, and were safely stored in the Castle of Brunswick. The personal belongings of the august household had been packed and were ready for immediate transportation. All running accounts had been settled and closed. What ready money there was left had been carefully collected and had been put up for convenient use by the fugitives. Remained the all-important question, "Where would they go?" Evidently no one at the court seems to have known. There still was a large British auxiliary army in the eastern provinces of the republic; but at the first approach of the French troops, the British soldiers had hastily crossed Gelderland and Overysel and had fled eastward toward Germany, a disorganized mob, burning and plundering as they went along to make up for the hardships of this terrible winter. Close at their heels followed the French army, strengthened by Dutch volunteers, guided by young Daendels, who knew his native province of Gelderland as he did the home town of Hattum. This time the young Patriot came as the conquering hero, and by the capture of the fortification of Heusden he cut off the road which connected the province of Holland with Germany.

To the north, to Helder, the road was still open. And the

fleet, assembled near Texel, was entirely dependable. But before William could make up his mind to go northward it was too late. The sudden surrender of Utrecht, the march of the French upon Amsterdam, cut off this second road, too. There remained but one way: to take ship in Scheveningen and flee to England. The only vessels now available were small fishing smacks, not unlike in form and rigging to the craft of the early vikings. The idea was far from inviting. The ships were bad sailers at all times. In winter they were positively dangerous. Now, however, these little vessels were all that was left, and to Scheveningen went the long row of carts, loaded with the goods of the small family and their half-dozen retainers, who were willing to follow them into exile. The end had come. The only question now was how to leave the stage with a semblance of dignity. William was passive to all that happened around him, accepting his fate with religious resignation. The Princess, a very grand lady, who would have smiled on her way to the scaffold, kept up an appearance of cheerful contempt.

Their two sons—William, the later King of Holland, and Frederick, who was to die four years later at the head of an Austrian army—vaguely attempted to create some military enthusiasm among the people; offered to blow themselves up in the last fortification. But what with ten thousand disorganized soldiers around them clamouring for food, for shoes, and for coats, it was no occasion for heroics. Why make sacrifices where nothing was to be gained? Despair and despondency, a shrugging of the shoulders and a protest, "What is the use?" met their appeal to the ancient courage and patriotism. Old Van den Spiegel, the last of the Raadpensionares, came nobly up to the best that was ever expected of his high office. He stuck to his duty until the very last. Day and night he worked. When too sick to go about he had himself carried on a litter into the meeting hall of the Estates. There he continued to lead the country's affairs and to give sound counsel until the moment the French entered The Hague and threw him into prison.

The Estates of Holland

On January the 17th the definite news of the surrender of Utrecht, of the imminent attack upon Amsterdam, and the approach of the French, had reached The Hague. It was a cold and sombre day. The people in a desultory curiosity flocked around the Stadholder's palace and the rooms of the Estates. A special mission had been sent to Paris several days before to offer the Committee of Public Safety a Dutch proposal of peace. The delegates, however, who had met with the opposition of the exiled Patriots who infested the French capital, had not made any headway, and for a long time they had been unable to send any news. The ordinary means of communication were cut off. The canal-boats could no longer run on account of the ice, and travel by land was slow. Any moment, however, their answer might be expected. But the 17th came and the 17th went by and not a word was heard from Paris. That night, in their ancient hall, in the dim light of flickering candles, the Estates General met to discuss whether the country could still be saved. Van den Spiegel was carried into the hall and reported upon the hopeless state of affairs. A committee of members was then appointed to inquire of his Highness whether he knew of a possible way out of the danger which was threatening the fatherland. Late that night the Prince received the deputies. A prolonged discussion took place. His Highness, alas! knew of no way out of the present difficulties. Unless the thaw should suddenly set in, unless the people should suddenly and spontaneously take up arms, unless Providence should directly intercede, the country was lost.

The next morning came, and still the frost continued, and not a single word of hopeful news. Panic seized the Estates. In all haste they sent two of their members to travel east, go find the commander of the invading army, and offer peace at any price. For when the French had attacked the republic they had proclaimed loudly that their war was upon the Stadholder as the tyrannous head of the nation, but not upon the nation itself. If that were the case, the Estates reasoned, let the nation sacrifice its ruler and escape further consequences. Wherefore, in their articles of capitulation, they did not mention the Stadholder. And from his side, William, who did not court martyrdom, declared nobly that he "did not wish to stand between the country's happiness and a continuation of the present struggle, and that he was quite ready to offer up his own interest and leave the land." In a lengthy letter to the Estates General he explained his point of view, took leave of his country, and recommended the rest to God.

During the night from Saturday to Sunday, January 17-18, 1795, the western storm which had been raging for almost a week subsided. An icy wind made the chance for flight to the English coast a possibility. Early in the morning the Princess Wilhelmina and her daughter-in-law, with a two-year-old baby, prepared for flight. Inside the palace, in the Hall of Audience, a room newly furnished at the occasion of her wedding, the Princess took leave of her few remaining friends. Many had already fled. Others, now that the French were within striking distance of the residence, preferred to be indisposed and stayed at home. Silently the Princess wished a farewell to her old companions. Outside the gate there was a larger assembly. Tradespeople grown gray in deep respect for their benefactors, simple folk whose political creed was contained in the one phrase "the House of Orange," Patriots wishing to see the last voyage of this proud woman, stood on both sides of the court's entrance. Nothing was said. It was no occasion for political manifestations. The two women and the baby, with a few servants following, slowly drove to Scheveningen. Without a moment's hesitation they were embarked, and at nine o'clock of the morning of this frightfully cold day they set sail for England. There, sick and miserable, they landed the next afternoon.

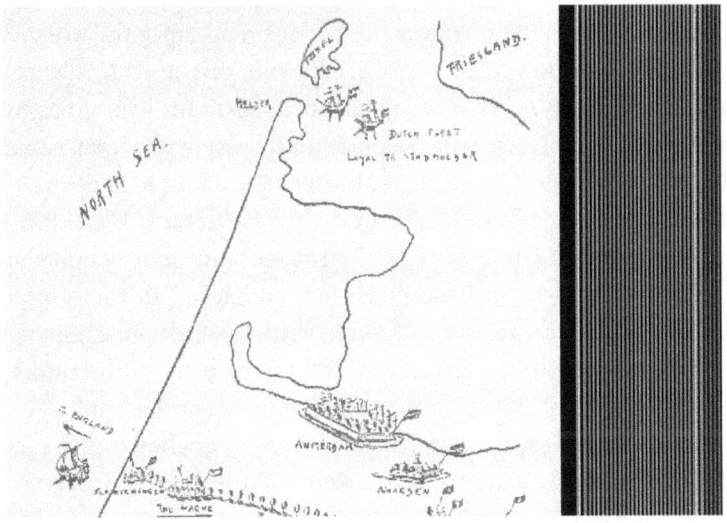

Flight of William V

At eleven o'clock the Prince heard that his wife had left in safety. The little palace in which he had built and rebuilt more than any of his ancestors was practically deserted. Outside, through force of habit, the sentinels of the Life Guard still trudged up and down and presented arms to the foreign ambassadors who drove up to take leave. The members of the Estates, in so far as they did not belong to the opposition, came in for a personal handshake and a farewell.

Poor William, innocent victim of his own want of ability, during these last scenes almost becomes a sympathetic figure. He tried to read a farewell message, but, overcome by emotion, he could not finish. A courtier took the paper and, with tears running down his face, read the last passages.

At half-past one the court carriages drove up for the final journey. By this time the whole city had made the best of this holiday and had walked out toward the road to Scheveningen.

Slowly, as if it meant a funeral, the long procession of carriages and carts wound its way over the famous road, once the wonder of its age, and now lined with curious folk, gazing on in silence, asking themselves what would happen next. In Scheveningen the shore was black with people; and everywhere that same ominous quiet as if some great disaster were about to happen. At two o'clock everything was ready for the departure. The Prince, with the young Duke of Hesse-Darmstadt and four gentlemen in waiting and his private physician, embarked in the largest ship. The other members of their suite were divided among some twenty little vessels, all loaded to the brim with trunks, satchels, bales of clothes, everything, in most terrible confusion. The situation was uncomfortable. To ride at anchor in the surf of the North Sea is no pleasure. And still the sign of departure was not given. Hoping against hope, the Stadholder expected to hear from the French authorities. At half-past four one of the members of the secret committee on foreign affairs of the Estates came galloping down to Scheveningen. News had been received from the French. It was unfavourable. The war was to continue until the Stadholder should have been eliminated.

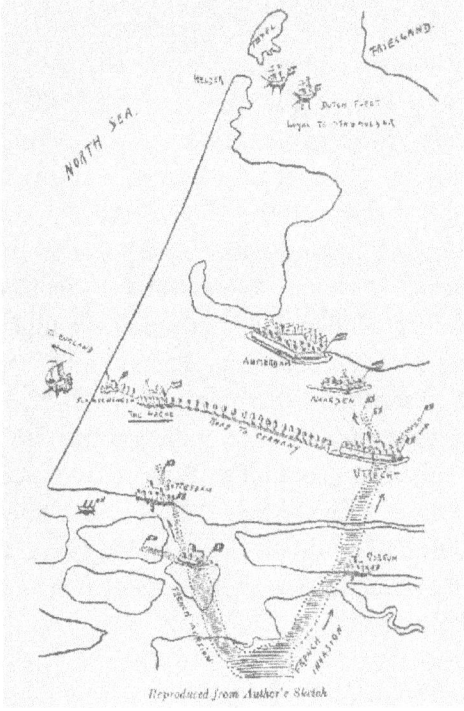

line map

The native fishermen—and they should have known what they were talking about—declared that every hour longer on this dangerous coast meant a greater risk. At any moment a boat manned with French troops might leave Rotterdam and intercept the fugitives. Furthermore, the sea was full of ice. The wind, which now was favourable, might change and blow the ice on the shore. They all advised his Highness to give the order to depart without further delay.

Whereupon William, in the cramped quarters of this smelly craft, in a sprawling hand, wrote his last official document. It reads like the excuses of a pouting child. "Really"—so he tells the Raadpensionaris—"really, since the French refuse an armistice, since there is no chance of reaching one or the other of the Dutch ports, really now, you cannot expect me to remain here aimlessly floating up and down in the sea forever." And then comes some talk of reaching Plymouth, where there "are a number of Dutch men-of-war, and of a speedy return to some Dutch province and to his good town of The Hague." All very nice and very commonplace and dilatory until the very end.

At five o'clock the ship carrying the Prince hoisted her sails. Before midnight William was well upon the high sea and out of all danger. The next morning, sick and miserable, he landed in Harwich. There the fishermen were paid off. Each captain received three hundred and fifty guilders. Then William wished them Godspeed and drove off to Yarmouth to meet his wife. It was the last time he saw so many of his countrymen. From now on he saw only a few individuals, exiles like himself, who visited him at his little court of Hampton and later at Brunswick, mostly asking for help which he was unable to give.

Exit at the age of forty-seven, William V, last hereditary Stadholder of the United Netherlands—a sad figure, intending to do the best, succeeding only in doing the worst; victim of his own weakness and of conditions that destroyed the strongest and the most capable. In the quiet atmosphere of trifling details and petty etiquette of a third-rate German princedom he ended his days. At his funeral he received all the honours and pomp to which his exalted rank entitled him. But he never returned to his own country.

Of all the members of the House of Orange William V is the only one whose grave is abroad.

Krayenhoff

II.

THE REVOLUTION

ÇA IRA.

Indeed and it will.

While William is still bobbing up and down on the uncomfortable North Sea, the republic, left without a Stadholder, left without the whole superstructure of its ancient government, is wildly and hilariously dancing around a high pole. On top of this pole is a hat adorned with a tricoloured sash. At the foot of the pole stands a board upon which is painted "Liberty, Fraternity, Equality." The music for the festivities is provided by the drums and fifes of the French soldiers. The melody that is being played is the "Marseillaise." Soon the Hollanders shall provide the music themselves to the tune of some 40,000,000 guilders a year. And they shall dance a gay little two-step across every battlefield of Europe.

The worst of the revolution of 1795, from our point of view, was its absolute sincerity and its great honesty of purpose. The modern immigrant approaching the shores of the promised land in total ignorance of what he is about to discover, but with a deep conviction that soon all will be well, is no more naïve and simple in his unwarranted optimism that was the good patriot who during the first months of the year 1796 welcomed the bedraggled French sansculottes as his very dear deliverers and put his best guestroom at the disposal of some Parisan tough in red, white, and blue pantaloons. Verily the millennium had come. Never, until within our own days of amateur sociology and of self-searching and devotion to the woes of our humbler brethren, has there been such conscientious desire to lift the world bodily out of its wicked old groove and put it upon a newer and better road. Whether this hysterical joy, this unselfish ecstasy, about a new life was founded upon a sound and tangible basis few people knew and fewer cared. The sacred fire burned in their breasts and that was enough.

It was no time for a minute analogy of inner sentiments. The world was all astir with great events ... *allons enfants de la Patrie,* and the devil take the hindmost.

Meanwhile, since in all enthusiasm, genuine or otherwise, there must be some method; since the music of brass bands does not fill empty stomachs, but a baker has to bake bread; since, to come to our point, the old order of things had been destroyed, but no state can continue without some sort of order—meanwhile, what was the exact status of this good land?

The French, as we have said before, had not made war upon the nation but upon the head thereof. Exit the head; remains the nation. What was the position of the latter toward their noble deliverers? This was a question which had to be decided at once. The moment the French soldiers should overrun the entire country and should become conquerors, the republic was liable to be treated as so much vanquished territory. The republic knew of other countries which had suffered a like fate and did not aspire to follow their example. Wherefore it became imperatively necessary to "do something." But what?

In The Hague, as a last nucleus of the old government, there remained a number of the members of the General Estates, deliberating without purpose, waiting without hope for some indication of the future French policy. Wait on, Your High and Mightinesses, wait until your fellow-members, who are now suing for peace, shall return with their tales of insult and contempt, to tell you their stories of an overbearing revolutionary general and of ill-clad ruffians, who are living on the fat of the land and refuse insolently to receive the honourable missionaries of the Most High Estates.

Of real work, however, of governing, meeting, discussing, voting, there will be no more for you to do. You may continue to lead an humble existence until a year later, but for the moment all your former executive power is centred in a body of which you have never heard before—in the Revolutionary Committee of Amsterdam.

The Revolutionary Committee in Amsterdam, what was it, whence did it come, what did it aspire to do? Its name was more formidable than its appearance. There were none of the approved revolutionary paraphernalia, no unshaven faces, nor unkempt hair. The soiled linen, once the distinguishing mark of every true Progressive, was not tolerated in this honourable company. It is true that wigs were discarded for man's own natural hair, but otherwise the leaders of this self-appointed revolutionary executive organ were law-abiding citizens, who patronized the barber regularly, who believed in the ancestral doctrine of the Saturday evening, and who had nothing in common with the prototypes of the French revolution but their belief in the same trinity of Liberty, Equality, and Fraternity, with perhaps a little less stress upon the Equality clause.

No, the Revolutionary Committee which stepped so nobly forward at this critical moment was composed of highly respectable and representative citizens, members of the best families. They acted because nobody else acted, but not out of a desire for personal glory. The army of personal glorifiers was to have its innings at a later date.

Now, let us try to tell what this committee did and how the old order of things was changed into a new one. After all, it was a very simple affair. A modern newspaper correspondent would have thought it just about good for two thousand words.

Warship Entering the Port of Amsterdam

On Friday, the 16th of January, the day on which the French took the town of Utrecht, a certain Wiselius, amateur author, writer of innumerable epics and lyrics, but otherwise an inoffensive lawyer and a member of the secret Patriotic Club, went to his office and composed an "Appeal to the People." In this appeal the people were called upon to "throw off the yoke of tyranny and to liberate themselves." On the morning of the 17th this proclamation, hastily printed, was spread throughout the town and was eagerly read by the aforementioned people who were waiting for something to happen. During the afternoon of the same day this amount of floating literature received a sudden and most unexpected addition. General Daendels, the man of the hour, commander of a battalion of Batavian exiles, while pushing on toward Amsterdam, had discovered a print-shop in the little village of Leerdam, and, in rivalry with Wiselius, he had set himself down to contrive another "Appeal to the People."

After a two hours' walk, his circulars had reached the capital and had breathed the genuine and unmistakable revolutionary atmosphere into the good town of Amsterdam. Here is a sample: "Batavians, the representatives of the French people demand of the Dutch nation that it shall free itself forthwith from slavery. They do not wish to come to the low countries as conquerors. They do not wish to force upon the old Dutch Republic the assignats which conquered territory must accept. (A fine bait, for this paper was money as valuable as Confederate greenbacks.) They come hither driven solely by the love of Liberty, Fraternity, and Equality, and they want to make the republic a friend and ally of France—an ally proud of her independence and her free sovereignty." When the Amsterdam Revolutionary Committee noticed the commotion made by these two proclamations, especially by the second one, it decided to act at once. Among the initiated inner circle the word was passed around that early the next morning, at the stroke of nine, a "Revolution" would take place. But before the arrival of the momentous hour many unexpected things happened. Let us try and explain them in due order.

On the afternoon of the 17th General Daendels had received a visit from an old friend, who was called Dr. Krayenhoff—an interesting type, possible only in the curious eighteenth century. Originally destined for the study of jurisprudence, he had drifted into medicine, had taken up the new plaything called electricity, and as an electrical specialist had made quite a reputation. From popular lectures upon electricity and the natural sciences in general he had drifted into politics, had easily become a leading member of the progressive part of the Patriots, and on account of his recognized executive ability had soon found himself one of the leaders of the party. He was a man of pleasant manners, rare personal courage, the combination of scientific, political, and military man which so often during the revolutionary days seemed destined to play a leading rôle. His former fellow-student, Daendels, who had been away from the country for more than eight years, had eagerly welcomed this ambulant source of information, and had asked Krayenhoff what chances of success the revolution would have in Amsterdam. The two old friends had a lengthy conversation, the result of which was that Krayenhoff declared himself willing to return to Amsterdam to carry an official message from Daendels to the town government and see what could be done. The town government was known to consist of weak brethren, and a little pressure and some threatening words might do a lot. There was only one obstacle to the plan of Daendels to march directly upon the capital. The strong fortification of Nieuwersluis was still in the hands of the troops of the old government. These might like to fight and block the way. But the commander of this post showed himself a man of excellent common sense. When Citizen Krayenhoff, on his way north, passed by this well-armed stronghold, the commander came out to meet him, and not only declared his eager intention of abandoning the fort but obligingly offered Mr. Krayenhoff a few of his buglers to act as parliamentaries on his expedition to Amsterdam.

Accordingly, on the morning of the 18th of January, Krayenhoff and his buglers appeared before the walls of the town, and in the name of the Franco-Batavian General Daendels proceeded to deliver their highly important message to their Mightinesses the burgomasters and aldermen. The message solemnly promised that there would be no shedding of blood, no destroying of property, no violence to the person; but it insisted in very precise terms upon an immediate revolution. All things would happen in order and with decency, but revolution there must be.

This summons to the town government was the sign for the Patriotic Club to make its first public appearance. Six of the most influential leaders of the party, headed by Rutger Jan Schimmelpenninck, incarnation of civic virtue and prudence, quietly walked to the town hall, where in the name of the people they demanded that the town government be delivered into their own hands.

Daendels

They assured the much frightened worthies of the town hall of their great personal esteem, and repeated the solemn promise that no violence of any sort would occur unless the militia be called out against them.

The gentlemen of city hall assured the Revolutionary Committee that violence was the very last thing which they had in mind. But of course this whole proceeding was very sudden. Would the honourable Revolutionary Committee kindly return at nine of that same evening, and then they would find everything arranged to their complete satisfaction. *Ita que acta.*

At half-past nine of the same evening the Revolutionary Committee returned to the town hall and found everything as desired. Krayenhoff, who was made military commander of the city, climbed on the stoop of the building and by the light of a torch held by one of his new soldiers he read to the assembled multitude a solemn proclamation which informed all present that a revolution had taken place, and that early the next morning the official exchange of the high government would take place.

French troops entering Amsterdam

After which the assembled multitude discreetly applauded and went home and to bed. The Revolutionary Committee, however, made ready for a night of literary activity and retired to the well-known inn, the Cherry Tree, to do a lot of writing. Soon paper and ink covered the tables and the work of composing proclamations was in full swing; but ere many hours had passed, who should walk in but our old friend Major-General Daendels. That afternoon while making a tour of inspection with a few French Hussars he had found the city gates of Amsterdam wide open and unguarded. Glad of the chance to sleep in a real bed, he had entered the town, had asked for the best hotel, and behold! our hero had been directed to the self-same Cherry Tree. His Hussars were made comfortable in the stable and he himself was asked to light a pipe and join his brethren in their arduous task of providing the literary background for a revolution.

The next morning, fresh and early, the French detachment drove up to form a guard of honour for the plain citizens who within another hour would be the official rulers of the city. When the clock of the New Church struck the hour of ten, the representatives of the people of Amsterdam entered the famous hall, where the town government had met in extraordinary session. Both parties exhibited the most perfect manners. The Patriots were received with the utmost politeness. They, from their side, assumed an attitude of much-distracted bailiffs who have come to perform a necessary but highly uncongenial duty. They assured the honourable town council again and again that no harm would befall them. But since (early the night before) "the Batavian people had resumed the exercise of their ancient sovereign rights," the old self-instituted authorities had been automatically removed and had returned to that class of private citizens from which several centuries before their ancestors had one day risen. The burgomaster and aldermen could not deny this fundamental piece of historical logic. They gathered up their papers, made a polite bow, and disappeared. The people assembled in the open place in front of the city hall paid no attention. Henceforth the regents could only have an interest as a historical curiosity. A new time had come. It was established upstairs, on the first floor, and another proclamation had been written. This first official document of the new era was then read from the balcony of the hall to the people below:

"Liberty, Fraternity, Equality. Fellow-Batavians: The old order of things has ceased to be. The new order of things will start with the following list of provisional representatives of the people of Amsterdam. (Follows a list of twenty-one names.) People of the Batavian Republic, what say ye?"

The people, patient audience in all such political entertainments, said what was expected of them. The twenty-one new dignitaries, thus duly installed, then took their seats upon the unfamiliar green cushions of the aldermanic chairs and went over to the order of the day. The former subjects, present citizens, still assembled in the streets, went home to tell the folks that there had been a revolution, and that, on the 20th of January of the first year of the Batavian liberty, the good town of Amsterdam had thrown off the yoke of tyranny and the people had become free. And at ten o'clock curfew rang and everybody went to sleep.

III.

THE COST OF REVOLUTION

This little historic comic opera which we are trying to compose has a great many "leitmotiven." The revolutionary ones are all of foreign make and importation. There is but one genuinely Dutch tune, the old "Wilhelmus of Nassau." But this we shall not hear for many, many years, until it shall be played by a full orchestra, with an extra addition of warlike bugles and the roaring of many cannon.

For the moment, while the overture is still being performed, we hear only a mumble of discordant and cacophonous Parisian street tunes. One melody, however, we shall soon begin to notice uppermost. It is the "Marseillaise," and it announces the approach of the taxpayer. For twenty years to come, whatever the general nature of our music, whenever we hear the strains of this inspiring tune, the villain of our opera will obey their summons and will make his rounds to collect from rich and poor with touching impartiality.

On Sunday, the 18th, the Stadholder left the country. On Monday, the 19th, the provisional representatives of the people of Amsterdam made their little bow to the people from the stoop of the town hall.

On the same day the French recognized the Batavian Republic officially. On Wednesday, the 21st, Amsterdam called upon fourteen other free cities to send delegates to discuss the ways and means of establishing a new government for the aforementioned republic. And on that same day the representatives of the French Republic unpacked their meagre trunks in the palace of the old

Stadholder and demanded an amount of supplies for the French army which would have kept the Dutch army in food and clothes and arms for half a dozen years.

The provisional authorities demurred. The bill was much too high. "But surely," the French delegates said, "surely you must comply with our wishes. We have marched all the way from Paris to this land of frogs to deliver you from a terrible tyrant. You can not expect us to starve." Of course not, and the supplies were forthcoming.

On the 26th of the same month, of January, the different provisional delegates from the provisional representative bodies of the different cities of Holland met in The Hague and sent word to the provincial Estates that their meeting hall was needed for different and better purposes. And when the old Estates had moved out the provisional citizens constituted themselves into an executive and legislative body, to be known as the "Provisional Representatives of the People of Holland."

The French authorities, snugly installed in the other wing of the palace where the provisionals met, were asked for their official approval. This they condescended to nod across the courtyard. Then the new representatives set to work. Pieter Paulus, our old friend of the Rotterdam Admiralty, was elected speaker, an office for which he was most eminently fitted. In his opening speech he touched all the strings of the revolutionary harp—peace, quiet, security, equality, safety, justice, humanity, fairness to all. Those were a few of the basic principles upon which the everlasting Temple of Civic Righteousness was to be constructed. After which the provisional meeting set to work, and in very short order abolished the office of Stadholder, the Raadpensionaris, the nobility, absolved every one from the old oath of allegiance, recalled the peace missionaries who were still supposed to be looking for the French authorities, and ended up with a solemn declaration of the Rights of Men and a promise immediately to convoke a national assembly. The other provinces followed Holland's example. In less than two weeks' time the entire country had dismissed its old Estates and had provided itself with a new set of rulers. The new machinery, as long as there was nothing to do but to demolish the ruins of the old republic, worked beautifully; but when the last stones had been carted away, then there was a very different story to tell.

Three weeks after the Stadholder had fled, provisional delegates to the Estates General (the name had been retained for convenience sake) met in The Hague. They adopted the Declaration of the Rights of Men as their ethical constitution, abolished for the whole country what the provisional provincial Estates had already abolished for each individual part, changed the five different admiralties into one single navy department, changed the Council of State into a committee-on-the general-affairs-of-the-Alliances-on-Land, and vested this committee with the short name with power to make preparations for the calling together of a National Assembly for the framing of a constitution.

And then—*allons enfants de la Patrie*—and here were those same citizens of the dilapidated uniform who had called but a moment before, and they had a little account which they would like to see settled. For now that the provisional delegates of the new republic were so conveniently together, would they not kindly oblige with a prompt payment? Poor Batavian Republic, while your provisional representatives are making speeches, while your people are eagerly trying to rid themselves of titles, honours, coats-of-arms, fancy wigs, and short trousers, while the entire Batavian Republic is stewing in a most delightful feeling of brotherly love, the good brethren in Paris are coldly calculating just how much they can take away from the republic without absolutely ruining her as a dividend-producing community.

The French national convention, in matters of a monetary nature, took no chances. It sent two of its best financial experts to Holland to make a close and first-hand inspection of all possible Dutch assets, and to study the relation between revenue and expenditure and to discover just how much bleeding this rich old organism could stand. On the 7th of February these two experts, the Citizens Ramel and Cochon (most fitting name), arrived in The Hague. In less than two weeks they were ready with their report. They certainly knew their business. "Do not kill the goose which lays the golden egg" was the tenor of their message to the French convention. "Let Holland prosper commercially, and then you shall be able to take a large sum every year for an unlimited number of years. But show some clemency for the present. Whatever there used to be of value in the republic has been sent abroad many months ago and now lies hidden in safety vaults in Hamburg and London. Reëstablish confidence. The rich will come back; their property will come back; dividends will come back. Then go in and take as much as the Dutch capital can stand."

Such was the gist of their advice, but it was very ill received by the triumvirate which conducted the foreign policy of the French Republic. They knew little of economics, but much about the pressing needs of the large armies which were fighting for the cause of Fraternity and Liberty. Money was needed in Italy and money was needed in Germany, and the republic must provide it. And to Citizen Paulus and his provisional assembly there went a summons for one hundred million guilders to be paid in cash within three months, and for a 3 per cent. loan of a same amount to be taken up by the Dutch bankers before the year should be over. Incidentally a vast tract of territory in the southern part of the republic was demanded to be used for French military purposes.

Here was a bit of constructive statesmanship for the month-old provisional government. Twenty-five thousand hungry French soldiers garrisoned in their home cities and a peremptory demand for two millions and several hundred square miles of land. Forward and backward the discussion ran. The republic was willing to open her colonies to French trade, to conclude an offensive and defensive treaty with France, to reorganize her fleet and use it against England. Not a cent less than a hundred millions, answered Paris.

The republic must not be driven to extremes, or France will lose all the influence which it has obtained so far.

"Go ahead," said Paris, "and get rid of us. The moment we shall recall our troops, the Prussians will come to reëstablish your little Stadholder the way they did in 1787. Our retreating army shall plunder all it can, and the rest will be left to the tender mercies of the Prussian's Hussars. Get rid of us and see what is to become of your Batavian Republic."

The Provisionals, recognizing the truth of this statement, fearing another restoration, asked time for deliberation. Then they offered to pay sixty millions and cede a vast tract of territory. "One hundred millions in cash and the same amount in a loan," said Paris, "and not a cent less."

Pieter Paulus (if only he had not died so young) worked hard and faithfully to try and avert this outrage. At times, as when he declared that "it were better to submit to the terms of a conqueror than to agree to such monstrous demands on the part of a professed friend," he rose to a certain heroism. But he stood alone, and his obstinate fight only resulted in a slight modification of some of the minor terms. One hundred millions in cash it was, and one hundred millions in cash it remained.

On the 16th of May, 1796, the treaty of The Hague was concluded between the French and the Batavian republics. The French guaranteed the independence and the liberty of the Batavian Republic and also guaranteed the abolition of the Stadholdership. Until the conclusion of a general European peace there should exist an offensive and defensive treaty between the two countries. Against England this treaty would be binding forever. Flushing must receive a French garrison. A number of small cities in the Dutch part of Flanders must become French. The colonies must be opened to French trade. The Dutch must equip and maintain a French army of 25,000 men, and fifty million guilders must be paid outright, with another fifty million to come in regular rates.

The Batavian Republic now could make up a little trial balance. This was the result:

Credit: the expulsion of one Stadholder and the establishment of a free republic; 2,365,000 guilders' worth of worthless paper money imported by the French soldiers. Debit: 50,000,000 in spot cash and 50,000,000 in future notes; 40,000,000 for French requisitions; 50,000,000 lost through passed English dividends, lost colonies, ruined trade. Total gain—Q.E.D.

IV.

THE PROVISIONAL

The provisional representatives of the people of Holland, the provisional representatives of the people of Zeeland, the provisional representatives of all the nine provinces (for the old generalities had been proclaimed into provinces), the provisional municipalities and provisional committees on the provisional revolution—the names indicate sufficiently the provisionally of the whole undertaking.

Curiously enough (but the contemporary of course could not know this) the Provisional government worked more and to a better effect than the permanent form of government by which it was followed. It had one great advantage: there was such an insistent demand for immediate action that there was a correspondingly small chance for idle talking. The professional orators, the silver-tongued rhetoricians, had their innings at a later date. For the moment only men of deeds were wanted, and the best elements of the Patriotic party cheerfully stepped forward to do their duty.

Pieter Paulus, by right of his ability, was the official and unofficial head. He remained at The Hague and ran the national Provisional government, while Citizen Schimmelpenninck stayed in Amsterdam and kept that important dynamo of democratic power running smoothly. Both leaders had their troubles, but not from foreign enemies. It is true that the young Prince of Orange was contemplating a wild filibustering scheme and had called for volunteers to compose an army of invasion. The half-pay officers of the former régime had hastened to his colours. But very few soldiers were willing to risk their lives for such an unpopular cause, and with an army composed of two soldiers for each officer no great military operations were possible. Wherefore the plan fell through in a most lamentable way, and the Prince of Orange as a claimant to the Dutch Government disappeared from further view until many years later.

The great bugaboo of the Provisional government and its moderate members was the radical brethren of the very same Patriotic party. These good people had starved abroad for many years. At the first opportunity they had hastened back to the ancestral hearth-stone. And now they presented enormous claims for damages for the losses which eight years before they had suffered at the hands of the Orangeists. But instead of receiving the hoped-for bounties these faithful democrats were snubbed on all sides. The climax was reached when the Batavian Government offered to pay them twenty-five guilders each (the price of a ticket from Paris to Amsterdam) and let it go at that. The professional exiles roared indignation, repaired to the nearest coffee-house, and instantly formed a number of clubs which were to see that no further deviations from the genuine path of revolutionary virtue be permitted. And very broadly they hinted that a short session of Madame Guillotine might do no end of good in this complacent and ungrateful Dutch community.

Let it be said to the everlasting honour of the Provisionals that no such thing occurred. Nobody was decapitated, no palaces and country houses were delivered to the tender mercies of the Jacobin Patriots.

The possessions of the Stadholder, which yielded 700,000 livres a year, were taken over by the republic and administered for its own benefit. The regents were permitted to exist, very, very quietly, and were not interfered with in any way. Yea, even when old Van den Spiegel and William's great friend Count Bentinck were brought to trial for malfeasance committed while in office they were immediately set free. And the citizen who conducted the investigation, Valckenaer by name and a most ardent Jacobin by profession, openly confessed that there had been no case against these two dignitaries, that the charges against them had been like spinach: "Looks like a lot when it is fresh, but does not make much of a dish when it gets boiled down."

No, the members of the Provisional were good Patriots and good democrats, but with all due respect for the doctrine of equality they did not aspire to that particular form of equality which is established by the revolutionary razor.

But after the question of the more turbulent members of their party had been decided, there was another problem of the greatest importance. Where, in the name of all the depleted treasuries, could the money be found with which to pay the French deliverers, the current expenses of this costly provisional government, the added sums necessary for the war with the enemies of France? The high sea was closed to Dutch trade, the colonies did not produce a penny's worth of revenue, Dutch industries were dead and buried under unpayable debts. Not a cent was coming in from anywhere; but whole streams of valuable guilders were flowing out of the country to everywhere.

The final solution of the problem was as simple as it was disastrous. The Batavian Republic began to live on the capital of the Dutch Republic. In some provinces the Provisional government confiscated all gold and silver with the exception of the plate used in the church service. But this little sum was gobbled up by the hungry treasury before a month was over. Then voluntary 5 per cent. loans were tried. They were not taken up. An extraordinary tax of 6 per cent. was levied upon all revenue. The money covered the running expenses for three weeks; and all the time those twenty-five thousand Frenchmen, who had to be clothed and fed, ate and ate and ate as if they had never seen a square meal before, which probably was the truth.

There was only one way out of the difficulty: The credit of the prodigal son, who for two centuries had regularly paid his bills, is apt to be good. The republic could loan as much as it wanted to, and it now abused this privilege. Loans were taken to pay dividends upon other loans, until finally a system was developed of loans within loans upon other loans which ultimately must ruin even the soundest of financial constitutions.

Meanwhile it poured assignats. All attempts to stop this unwelcome shower at its source were met with the most absolute refusal of the French Government. "What! dishonour our pretty greenbacks with their fine mottoes, and accepted everywhere as the true badges of good revolutionary faith?" They could not hear of such a thing. And they printed assignats, and the counterfeiters printed assignats, and every private citizen whose children owned a little private printing press and whose oldest boy knew the rudiments of drawing printed assignats, until the shower caused a deluge, which in due time swamped the whole financial district and brought about that horror of horrors—a national bankruptcy.

Enters No. 3 upon the program of the Provisional's difficulties: the army and the navy.

Daendels had obtained permission to leave the French service and had assumed command of the Dutch troops. A strange conglomeration of troops, by the way, not unlike the mercenary armies of the Middle Ages: regiments composed of every nationality—Swiss grenadiers and Saxon cavalry, Scotch life guards and Mecklenburg chasseurs, a few Dutch engineers and some Waldeck infantry; the officers partly Dutch, but mostly foreign; the higher officers mostly in exile; the lower ones awaiting the day when their friend the Prince should return. Surely before this army could be reorganized into a national army of 24,000 well-equipped men, hot-blooded Daendels would have a chance to exercise that swift temper of his. For after a year of drilling there was not even a single company that could be depended upon in a regular skirmish in time of war.

With the fleet the government did not experience such very great difficulties. The fifteen millions necessary for reorganization had been quickly collected, and Paulus a specialist on this subject, had gone to work with a will. The old officers and men had either left the service, or had surrendered their ships to the English as the allies of their commander-in-chief, the Stadholder. But there were enough sailors in the country to man the ships. Such of the old ships as had remained in Dutch harbours were rebaptized with more appropriate names—the *William the Silent* became the *Brutus*, the *Estates General* was renamed the *George Washington*, and the *Princess Wilhelmina* was delicately changed to the *Fury*—and twenty-four new ships of the line and twenty-four frigates were planned for immediate construction.

After half a year Admiral de Winter (former second lieutenant of the navy and French general of infantry) was ready to leave Texel with the first Batavian fleet. He sailed from Texel with a couple of ships, and after having been beaten by an English squadron off the coast of Norway, he returned to Texel with a few ships less. Two special squadrons were then equipped and ordered to proceed to the West and East Indian Colonies; but before they left the republic news was received of the conquest of these colonies by the British, and the auxiliary squadrons were given up as useless.

Now all these puzzling questions facing untrained politicians took so much of their time that nothing was apparently done toward the great goal of this entire revolution—the establishment of a national assembly to draw up a constitution and put the country upon a definite legitimate basis.

The country began to show a certain restlessness. The old Orangeists smiled. "They knew what all this desultory business meant. Provisional, indeed? Provisional for all times." The more extreme Patriots, who knew how sedition of this sort was preached all over the land, showed signs of irritation. "It was not good that the opposition could say such things. Something must be done and be done at once. Would the Provisional kindly hurry?"

But when the Provisional did not hurry, and when nothing was done toward a materialization of the much-heralded constitution, the Jacobins bethought themselves of what they had learned in their Parisian boarding school and decided to start a lobby—a revolutionary lobby, if you please; not a peaceful one which works in the dark and follows the evil paths of free cigars and free meals and free theatre tickets. No, a lobby with a recognized standing, a clubhouse visible to all, and rules and by-laws and a well-trained army of retainers to be drawn upon whenever noise and threats could influence the passing of a particular bill.

On the 26th of August, 1795, there assembled in The Hague more than sixty representatives from different provincial patriotic clubs. The purpose of the meeting was "to obtain a national assembly for the formation of a constitution based upon the immovable rights of men—Liberty and Equality—and having as its direct purpose the absolute unity of this good land." Here at last was a program which sounded like something definite—"the absolute unity of this land."

All the revolutionary doings of the last six months, the patriotic turbulences of the past generation, were not as extreme, as anti-nationalistic in their outspoken tendencies, as was this one sentence: "The absolute unity of this land." It meant "Finis" to all the exaggerated provincialism of the old republic. It meant an end to all that for many centuries had been held most sacred by the average Hollander. It meant that little potentates would no longer be little potentates, but insignificant members of a large central government. It meant that the little petty rights and honours for which whole families had worked during centuries would pale before the lustre of the central government in the capital. It meant that all High and Mightinesses would be thrown into one general melting-pot to be changed into fellow citizens of one undivided country. It meant the disappearance of that most delightful of all vices, the small-town prejudice. And all those who had anything to lose, from the highest regent down to the lowest village lamplighter, made ready to offer silent but stubborn resistance. To give up your money and your possessions was one thing, but to be deprived of all your little prerogatives was positively unbearable. And not a single problem with which the Provisional, or afterward the national assembly, had to deal, caused as many difficulties as the unyielding opposition of all respectable citizens to the essentially outlandish plan of a single and undivided country.

As a matter of fact, the unity was finally forced upon the country by a very small minority. The Dutch Jacobins were noisy, they were ill-mannered, and on the whole they were not very sympathetic. (Jacobins rarely are except on the stage.) But one thing they did, and they did it well. By hook and by crook, by bullying, and upon several occasions by direct threats of violence, they cut the Gordian knot of provincialism and established a single nation and a union where formerly disorganization and political chaos had existed. For when their first proposal of the 26th of August was not at once welcomed by the Provisional, the revolutionary lobbyists declared themselves to be a permanent Supervisory Committee, and as the "Central Assembly" (of the representatives from among the democratic clubs of the Batavian Republic) they remained in The Hague agitating for their ideas until at last something of positive value had been accomplished.

The Estates General could refuse to receive communications from this self-appointed advisory body, the Estates of a number of provinces could threaten its members with arrest, but here they were and here they stayed (in an excellent hotel, by the way, which still exists and is now known as the Vieux Doelen), sitting as an unofficial little parliament, and fighting with all legitimate and illegitimate means for the fulfilment of their self-imposed task. And one year and one month after the glorious revolution which we have tried to describe in our previous chapters, the provisional assembly, under the influence of these ardent Patriots and their gallery crowd, decided to call together a "national assembly to draw up a constitution and to take the first steps toward changing the fatherland into a united country."

And this is the way they went about it: The national assembly should be elected by all Hollanders who were twenty years of age. They must be neither paupers nor heretics upon the point of the people's sovereignty. For the purpose of the first election, the provinces were to be divided into districts of 15,000 men each, subdivided into sub-districts of 500. The sub-districts, voting secretly and by majority of votes, were to elect one elector and one substitute elector. The elector must be twenty-five years of age, not a pauper, and a citizen of four years' standing. Thirty electors then were to elect one representative and two substitute representatives. These must be thirty years of age and were to represent the people in the national assembly. Their pay was to be four dollars a day and mileage. The national convention was to be an executive and legislative body after the fashion of the Estates General during those old days when no Stadholder had been appointed. Within two weeks after its first meeting the national assembly must appoint a suitable commission of twenty-one members (seven from Holland, one from Drenthe, and two from each of the other provinces). Said commission, within six months of date, must draw up a constitution. This constitution then must at once be submitted to the convention for its approval, and within a year it must be brought before the people for their final referendum.

The elections actually took place in the last part of February of the year 1796. They took place in perfect order and with great dignity. The system was not exactly simple, but it was something new, and it was rather fun to study out the complicated details and then walk to the polls and exercise your first rights as a full-fledged citizen.

On the 1st of March more than half of the representatives, duly elected, assembled in The Hague, ready to go to work.

A year had now gone by since the provisional government had been started—a year which had little to show for itself except an ever-increasing number of debts and an ever-decreasing amount of revenue. The time had come for the direct representatives of the sovereign people to indicate the new course which inevitably must bring to the country the definite benefits of its glorious but expensive revolution.

Exit the provisional assembly and enter the national assembly.

V.

SOLEMN OPENING OF THE NATIONAL ASSEMBLY THE OPENING CEREMONIES

On the morning of the 1st of March, 1796, the ever-curious people of The Hague had a legitimate reason for taking an extra holiday. For two weeks carpenters, plumbers, and whitewashers, followed by paperhangers and upholsterers, had been at work in the former palace of the Stadholder. They had hammered and papered until the former ballroom of Prince William V had been changed into a meeting room for the new national assembly. It was an oblong room eighty by thirty-two feet, and extremely high. The members were to sit on benches behind tables covered with the obligatory green baize. Their benches were built in long rows, four deep, constructed along three sides of the hall and facing the windows which gave on the courtyard. The centre part of the fourth wall, between the big windows, was taken up by a sort of revolutionary throne, which was to be occupied by the Speaker and his secretaries. The chair of the Speaker was a ponderous affair, embellished with wooden statues representing Liberty and Fraternity. The gallery for the people, one of the most important parts of a modern assembly hall, gave room for three hundred citizens. The principle of equality, however, had not been carried to such an extreme as in the French assemblies. There was a separate gallery for the use of the diplomats and the better class of citizens. Unfortunately there were but few diplomats left to avail themselves of this opportunity to listen to Batavian rhetoric. Practically all of the foreign ministers had left The Hague soon after the Prince had departed.

The members of the assembly, after the French fashion, were not to speak from their seats, but when they wished to address their colleagues and the nation they mounted a special little pulpit standing on the right of the Speaker's throne and resembling (or trying to resemble) a classical rostrum.

Now let us tell what the good people of The Hague were to see on this memorable 1st of March. All in all there were ninety-six representatives in town, and they came from seven provinces.

Friesland and Zeeland, neither of which liked the idea of this assembly, which was forced upon them by a revolutionary committee, had purposely delayed their elections—had not even commenced with the preliminaries of the first election. The other provinces, however, especially Drenthe and the former Generalities, which for the first time in their history acted as independent bodies, had been eager to go to work, and at eleven o'clock of this 1st of March their representatives and their substitutes, in their Sunday best, came walking to their new quarters. Slowly they gathered, until at the stroke of noon just ninety members were present. Punctually at that moment a delegation appeared from across the way, from the Estates General. They were to be the godfathers of the new assembly. Nine members of the old Estates General, escorted by a guard of honour from among the assembly, filed into the hall and took special seats in front of the Speaker's chair. One of them then read the names of the assemblymen whose credentials had been examined and had been passed upon favourably. The new members then drew lots for their seats. This ceremony was to be repeated every two weeks and was to prevent the formation of a Mountain and a Plain and other dangerous geographical substances fatal to an undisturbed political cosmos. The substitute representatives took their seats on benches behind their masters. Then the chairman of the delegation from across the way read a solemn declaration, which took the place of the former oath of allegiance, and the representatives expressed their fidelity to this patriotic pledge. The chairman ended this part of the ceremony with a fine outburst of rhetoric in which the Spanish tyranny, King Philip the second, Alva, the dangerous ambition of William of Nassau, and the spirit of liberty of the Batavian people passed in review before his delighted hearers. And having dispatched the odious tyrant, William V, across the high seas, he referred to the blessings that were now to flow over the country, and thanked the gentlemen for their kind attention.

The next subject on the program was the election of a Speaker. At the first vote Pieter Paulus, with 88 votes against 2, was elected Speaker of the Assembly. The chief delegate from the Estates General, in his quality of best man at this occasion, put a tricoloured sash across the shoulders of Mr. Paulus and conducted him to the Speaker's chair. Profound silence. The galleries, crowded to the last seat, held their breath. The ministers from the French Republic and the United States of America, who, with the diplomatic representatives of Denmark and Portugal, were the only official foreigners present, looked at their watches that they might inform their home governments at what moment exactly the new little sister republic had started upon her career.

It was twelve o'clock when Citizen Paulus arose and with a firm voice declared: "In the name of the people of the Netherlands, which has duly delegated us to our present functions, I declare this meeting to be the Representative Assembly of the People of the Netherlands."

Tremendous applause. A band hidden in a corner struck up a revolutionary hymn. Outside a bugle call announced unto the multitudes that the new régime had been officially established. The soldiers presented arms. The populace hastened to embrace the soldiers and to give vent to such expressions of civic joy as were fashionable at that moment. The national flag, the old red, white, and blue with an additional Goddess of Liberty, was hoisted on the highest available spot, which happened to be a little observatory where the children of the Stadholder in happier days had learned to read the wonders of the high heavens. The appearance of this flag was the appointed signal for those who had not been able to find room in the small courtyard, and they now burst forth into cheers. Finally the cannon, well placed outside the city limits (to avoid accidents to careless patriotic infants), boomed forth their message, and those who possessed a private blunderbuss fired it to their hearts' content. Ere long dispatch riders hastened to all parts of the country and told the glorious news.

The committee from the Estates General, however, did not wait for this part of the celebration. As soon as Paulus had begun his inaugural address (a quiet and dignified document, much to the point) they had unobservedly slipped out of the assembly and had returned to their own meeting hall across the yard. And here, while outside in the streets the people went into frantic joy about the new Batavian liberty, their High and Mightinesses, who for so many centuries had conducted the destinies of their own country and who so often had decided the fate of Europe, who had appointed governors of a colonial empire stretching over many continents, and who, chiefly through their own mistakes, had lost their power—here, their High and Mightinesses met for the very last time. The committee which had attended the opening of the Representative Assembly of the People of the Netherlands reported upon what they had done, what they had seen, and what they had heard. Then with a few fitting words their speaker closed the meeting. Slowly their High and Mightinesses packed up their papers and dispersed. Outside the town prepared for illumination.

Pieter Paulus

VI.

PIETER PAULUS

A year before, the French Revolution had come suddenly, and boldly it had struck its brutal bayonet into the industrious ants' nest of the Dutch Republic. There had been great hurrying to save life and property. After a while order had been reëstablished. And then to its intense surprise, at first with unbelieving astonishment, later with ill-concealed vexation, the political entymologists of the French Revolution had discovered that in this little country they had hit upon an entirely new variety of national fabric. Against all the rules of well-conducted republics, every little ant and every small combination of ants worked only for its own little selfish ends, disregarded its neighbours, fought most desperately for every small advantage to its own, bit at those who came near, stole the eggs of those who were not looking—in a word, while outwardly the little heap of earth seemed to cover a well-conducted colony of formicidæ, inwardly it appeared to be an ill-conducted, quarrelsome congregation of very selfish little individuals. And with profound common sense, the French, after their first surprise was over, said: "Brethren, this will never do. Really you must change all this. We will give you a chance to build a new nest, a very superior one. You can upholster it just as you please. You can put in all the extra outside and inside ornaments which you may care to have around you. But you must stop this insane quarrelling among yourselves, this biting at each other, this spoiling of each other's pleasure. In one word, you have got to turn this chaotic establishment of yours into a well-regulated, centralized commonwealth such as is now being constructed by all modern nations."

Very well. But who was to perform the miracle? William the Silent had failed. Oldenbarneveldt two hundred years before had told his fellow citizens almost identically the same thing. John de Witt had tried to bring about a union by making the whole country subservient to Holland, but he had not been successful. William III had accomplished everything he had set out to do, but he could not establish a centralized government in the republic. The entire eighteenth century had been one prolonged struggle to establish the beginning of a more unified system, and in this struggle much of the strength and energy of the country had been wasted in vain.

And now the untrained national assembly (Representative Assembly of the People of the Netherlands was too long a word) was asked to perform a task which was to make it odious to more than half of its own members and to the vast majority of the people of the republic.

Revolution, sansculottes, assignats, carmagnole, unpowdered hair—the Batavians were willing to stand for almost anything, but not one iota of provincial sovereignty must be sacrificed.

Pieter Paulus, wise man of this revolution, knew and understood the difficulties which were awaiting him and his assembly. Already, in his inaugural address, he had warned the members of the assembly that they must not forget to be "representatives of the whole people, not mere delegates from some particular town or province." The members had listened very patiently, but when, on the 15th of the month, the commission for the drawing up of a constitution was elected, the federalists, those who supported the idea of provincial sovereignty as opposed to a greater union, proved to be in the majority.

Of the twenty-one members who were elected to make a constitution, only one was known as a radical supporter of the idea of union. Since Zeeland and Friesland, even at this advanced date, had not yet sent their delegates, the commission could not commence its labours until the end of April. And when at last they set to work the assembly had suffered an irreparable loss. One week after the opening ceremonies the secretary of the assembly had asked that Mr. Paulus be excused from presiding that day. A heavy cold had kept him at home. Paulus was still a young man, only a little over forty. But during the last fourteen months, almost without support, he had carried the whole weight of the revolutionary government. And as soon as the assembly had met, the disgruntled Jacobins, who thought that he was not radical enough, had openly accused him of financial irregularities. It is true the assembly had refused to listen to these charges and the members had expressed their utmost confidence in the speaker; but eighteen hours' work a day, the responsibility for a State on the verge of ruin, and attacks upon his personal honesty, seemed to have been too much for a constitution which never had been of the strongest. The slight cold which had prevented Paulus from presiding proved to be the beginning of the end. After the 6th of March the speaker no longer appeared in the assembly. On the 15th of the same month he died.

The greatest compliment to his abilities can be found in the fact that after his death the national assembly at once degenerated into an endless debating society which, in imitation of the Roman Senate, deliberated and deliberated until not merely Saguntum, but the country itself, the colonies, and the national credit had been lost, and until once more French bayonets had to be called upon to establish the order which the people seemed to be unable to provide for themselves.

The National Assembly

VII.

NATIONAL ASSEMBLY NO. I AT WORK

The revolutionists in Holland had not followed the example of the French in abolishing the Lord. All denominations received full freedom of worship, and, faithful to an old tradition, the meetings of the assembly were invariably opened with prayer. As an ideal text for this daily supplication one of the members of the assembly offered the following invocation, short and much to the point: "O Lord, from trifling, dilly-dallying, and procrastination save us now and for ever-more. Amen."

Posterity seconds this motion.

The temple of national liberty became an elocution institute where beribboned and besashed members idled their time away making heroic speeches for the benefit of some ancestral Buncomb County.

Let us be allowed to use a big word—the Psychological Moment. The leaders of the revolution had allowed this decisive moment to go by, and the day came when they were to pay dearly for their negligence. If, immediately after the flight of the Prince in the first glory of victory, they had dared to declare the old order of things abolished, if they had trusted themselves sufficiently to abrogate the union of Utrecht, to annul the provincial sovereignty and destroy the old power of the provincial Estates, they could, assisted by the French armies, have transformed the old republic into a new united nation. But a century of vacillation and indecision had ill prepared them for such a decisive step. The Amsterdam Patriots, trained in the energetic school of a commercial city, wanted to go ahead and draw the consequences of their first act. But the other cities had not dared to go as far as that. And now, after a year of hesitation, it was too late. Radicalism was no longer fashionable. The old conservative spirit momentarily subdued, but by no means dead, had had three hundred and sixty-five days in which to regain its hold on the mass of the people. Incessantly, although guardedly, the conservatives kept up their agitation against a united country. "Unity merely means the leadership of Holland." This became the political watchword of all those who were opposed to the Patriots. "Unity will mean that our dear old sovereign provinces will have to take orders from some indifferent official in The Hague. Unity will mean that we all shall pay an equal share in the country's expenses and that Holland, with its majority of 400,000 inhabitants, will pay no more than the smallest province." And with all the stubbornness of people defending a losing cause, the old regents fought this terrible menace of a united country. They fought it in the market-place and in the rustic tavern. They offered resistance in every town hall and in the national assembly. Every question which entered the assembly (and questions and bills and decrees entered this legislative body by the basketful) was looked at from this one single point of view, was discussed with this idea uppermost in people's minds, and finally was decided in a way which would work against the unity of the country and the leadership of Holland. The acts of the national assembly fill eight large quartos; the decrees issued by the national assembly fill twenty-three. Certainly here was no lack of industry. Every imaginable question was touched upon by this enthusiastic body of promising young statesmen. Every conceivable problem, however difficult, was discussed with ease and eloquence. The separation of Church and State, something which has baffled statesmen for many centuries, was number one upon the new program. The sluices of oratory were opened wide. Each member in turn came forward with his observations. Nor did he confine himself to a few words directed to the Speaker of the assembly. No—a speech to the entire nation, to say the very least—a speech divided and subdivided in paragraphs like a Puritan sermon and delivered in the most approved pulpit style, sacred gestures, nasal twang, and all. At times, such as when the clown of the assembly (appropriately named Citizen Chicken) went forth to talk down the rafters of the ancient building, the Speaker tried to put a stop to the overflow of eloquence.

But the speakership was a movable office. Every two weeks the entire assembly changed seats and elected a new Speaker. By voting for the right kind of man (from their point of view) the loquacious majority could always arrange matters in such a way that their stream of babbling oratory was kept unchecked. In August, after a lengthy debate, the separation of Church and State was made a fact. Immediately thereupon a law was passed giving the franchise to the Jews. Eighty thousand citizens of the Hebrew persuasion now obtained the right to vote. Another grave problem, agitated for more than fifty years, was the creation of a national militia. Theoretically everybody was in favour of it. In practice, however, most Hollanders would rather dig ditches than play at soldier. The definite abolition of the uncountable mediæval feudal rights which in the year 1795 covered the country in a most complicated maze then came in for prolonged discussion.

Most painful of all, because most disastrous to the pockets of the people, was the question of what should be done with the East India Company. This ancient institution, threatened for several years with bankruptcy, must in some way be provided for. While finally the problem of a new system of national finances, satisfactory to all the provinces, was to engage the discordant attention of the assembly.

The speaker of the Assembly welcoming the French Minister

In some of these important matters decisions were actually reached. Others were discussed in endless tirades, full of repetition and reiteration. If the point at issue was too obscure to be clearly understood by the majority of the members, it was usually referred to the commission on the constitution, which as some sort of superior being was expected to solve all difficulties satisfactorily at some vague future date. Or, better still, it was put upon the table until that happy day when the constitution should actually have become a fact, and when a regular parliament, elected along strictly constitutional lines, should have been called together. This famous committee on the constitution was supposed to meet in executive session, but, not unlike the executive sessions of another renowned body of legislators, the discussions which had taken place during the morning and afternoon were generally known among the newspaper correspondents the same evening. And those among them who had maintained hopes of a united fatherland must have been sorely disappointed when week after week they reported the proceedings of the secret sessions and noticed how the little constitution under the tender care of its federalistic guardian was being clothed with a suit of a most pronounced federal hue, cut after a pattern designed by the most provincial of political tailors. On the 10th of November, 1796, the little infant constitution was first presented to the admiring gaze of the national assembly. The federalists were delighted. The unionists denounced it as the work of traitors, of disguised Orangemen, of reactionaries of the very worst sort. Undoubtedly the unionists and the Patriots had a right to be angry. This new constitution was a mere variation of the old republican theme of the year 1576, the year of the union of Utrecht. The Stadholdership was abolished. The executive power was now invested in a council of state consisting of seven members. The old Estates General was discontinued. In its place there was to appear an elected parliament consisting of two chambers and provided with legislative powers. The old provinces were abolished, but under the new name of departments they retained their ancient sovereignty and remained in the possession of all their old rights and prerogatives. That was all.

The political clubs were furious. The Jacobins rattled the knives of imaginary guillotines. The gallery of the assembly became filled with wild-eyed patriots. The assembly, somewhat frightened by the popular storm of disapproval, burst forth into speech and talked for eleven whole days to prove that really and truly this constitution was not a return to the old days, that it was most up-to-date and promised to the country a new and brilliant future. Then, when this oratory did not appease the popular anger even after fully two thirds of the members had favoured the occasion with their personal observations, the assembly gave in and solemnly promised to do some more trimming. Back the little constitution went to its original guardians, who were reinforced by ten other members and who had special instructions to put the child into a newer and more popular garb. This process of rejuvenation took six months. The committee of twenty-one did its best, but old traditions proved to be too strong. On the 30th of May, 1797, the national assembly by a large majority adopted the federalistic constitution and at once sent it to the electors for their final decision. Two years of work of enormous expense and sore defeat had gone by. As a result the assembly had produced a constitution which did not remove a single one of the faults of the former system of government, but added a few new ones. In August the session of the first national assembly was closed. Three weeks later the constitution was presented to the sovereign people for their consideration. Of those entitled to vote almost three fourths stayed at home. Of the remaining one hundred and thirty thousand voters five out of every six declared themselves against the constitution. The noes had it.

VIII.

NATIONAL ASSEMBLY NO. II AT WORK

There could be no doubt about the views of the majority of the people who took an interest in active politics. In unmistakable tones they had declared in favour of unionism. When the new election came they hastened to the polls and elected into the new assembly a large majority of unionists. Such was their enthusiasm that several of the more prominent unionist leaders were elected by seven and twelve electoral colleges at the same time. In this new assembly the moderate party, which had been the centre of the first one and which had counted among its members some of the best-trained political minds, was no longer present. Its leaders had not considered it worth the while. The unionists in the first assembly had claimed that the moderates by supporting the federalists had been directly responsible for the failure of the first constitution. "All right," the moderates said, "let the unionists now try for themselves and see what they can do." And the moderates stayed quietly at home and resumed their law practice. For most of these excellent gentlemen were lawyers and had offices needing their attention. On the whole their decision was a wise one.

When a serious operation has to be performed, philosophic doctors who start upon an academic discussion of the patient's chances of recovery are not wanted. And certainly, since the great day of the abjuration of King Philip II in the year 1581, the country had not passed through any such violent crisis as it was now facing. The big French brother, heartily disgusted with this dilatory business, this trifling away of so much valuable time, hinted more clearly than ever before that something definite must be done and must be done quickly. A new government must be constructed by men who not only strongly believed in themselves but also in the efficacy of their measures and the sacredness of their cause. If no such men could be found it were better indeed if France should import a ready-made constitution and should perform the task for which the Hollanders themselves seemed so ill fitted.

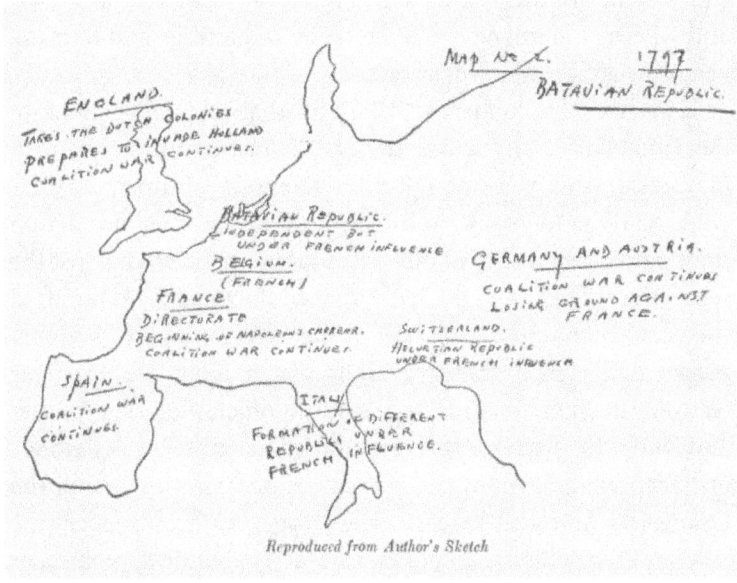

1797 Batavian Republic

On September 1, 1797, the second assembly met. The constitutional committee of twenty-one was duly elected, and the representatives set to work. So did the patriotic clubs. By constant agitation they reminded the representatives in The Hague that what the people wanted was a unionistic constitution, not another mild dilution of the old-fashioned rule of the regent. Every little outburst of Orangeistic sentiment—a drunken sailor hurrahing for the Prince, a half-witted peasant mumbling rumours of another Prussian restoration—was used as an excuse for new petitions, for ponderous memoranda to be addressed to the national assembly and to be presented by some patriotic member with a few well-chosen and trenchant words.

Came the defeat of the fleet by the British—discussed in the next chapter—and the inevitable cry of treason to increase the general confusion. The clubs knew all about it. The country was full of traitors who were secretly devoted to the Prince and wished to return to William his old dignities and to bring vengeance upon all pure Patriots.

Had not the Reformed Church—that old stronghold of the House of Orange—had not the Reformed ministers, with pious zeal, been working upon the religious sentiment of their congregations for weeks and months, and had they not driven their parishioners to the bookstores to sign petitions against the separation of Church and State? Indeed they had! Two hundred thousand men, more than half of the total number of national voters, had signed those petitions which must prevent their beloved ministers from losing their old official salaries. Louder and louder the patriotic minority wailed its doleful lamentations of treachery; and more and more firm became the tone of the Orangeists and the reactionaries. You see, dear reader, the revolution by this time had proved a terrible disappointment to most people. Under the old order of things there had been great economic and political disasters. But then there had been a Stadholder to be held responsible and to be made into the official scapegoat. Enter the Patriot with the advice, "Remove the Stadholder, establish the sovereignty of the people, and politically, economically, and socially all will be well." Very well. The Stadholder had been chased into the desert; the sovereignty of the people had been established. Then everybody had gone back to his business, trusting that the people's supreme power, like some marvellous patent medicine, would automatically take care of all the necessary improvements. Quite naturally nothing of the sort had happened. Of all the different systems of government—and even the best of them are but a makeshift—intended to bring comfort to the average majority, there is nothing more difficult to institute or to maintain than a sovereignty of all the people. It needs endless watching. It is a big affair which touches everybody. It is subject to more attacks from without and from within, to more onslaughts from destructive political parasites, than any other form of government. Take the case of the Batavian Republic. First of all, the hungry exiles of the year 1787 had descended upon its treasury to still their voracious appetites. Then the serious-minded lawyers had interfered and had said: "No, we must go about this work slowly and deliberately. We must first read up on the subject. We must peruse all the books and all the pamphlets written about assemblies and constitutions and natural rights, and then we must draw our own conclusions." Next, the federalists, desiring to save what could be saved from the wreck of their beloved government, had tried to undo all the work of the Patriots by their own little insiduous methods.

No, as a general panacea for all popular ailments the sovereignty of a people had not yet proved itself to be a success. And then, the cost! O ye gods! the bad assignats—the millions of guilders for the requisitions of the French army, the other millions to be paid in taxes for the support of the new government! And the results—the destruction of the fleet, the loss of almost all the colonies, the complete annihilation of trade and commerce! While as the only tangible result of all this effort there were the thirty-one ponderous volumes of the assemblies' speeches and decrees.

Perhaps, when all was said and done, was it not better to look the facts boldly in the face and return to the old order of things? Ahem and Aha! Perhaps it was. It must not be said too loudly, however, for the patriotic clubs might hear it, and they were a wild lot. "But now look here, brother citizen, what have you as a plain and sensible man gained by this assembly and by all this election business? Have you paid a cent less in taxes? No. Have your East Indian bonds increased in value? No. They are not worth a cent to-day. Have you found that your commerce was better protected than before? No. The fleet has never been in a worse condition than it is now." And so on, and so on, *ad infinitum*. The patriotic clubs of course knew that such an agitation was abroad throughout the land. They knew that the trees of liberty had long since been cut into firewood by shivering citizens; they knew that in many an attic the housewife had inspected her old supply of Orange ribbons and had hopefully provided them with fresh mothballs. And they knew that with another six months of the present bad government their last chance at power would have gone. Therefore, as apt pupils of the French Revolution, they bethought themselves of those remedies which the French used to apply on similar occasions. Had not the great republic of the south just expurgated her own assembly of all those traitors who under the guise of popular representatives had secretly professed royalism, Catholicism, and every sort and variety of anti-revolutionary and reactionary doctrines? Was not the new French directory there to prove to all the world that France was still the same old France of five years ago and had no intention of again submitting to the ancient royalistic yoke? And had not the Batavian Club celebrated this great event with much feasting and toasting, and had it not sent delegates to Paris to compliment the directors upon the brilliant success of their great coup? Glorious France had given the example. The free Batavians could but admire and follow. The French *coup d'état* of the 4th of September, 1797, was followed by the Dutch *coup d'état* of the 22nd of June, 1798. But the Dutch one, with all the satisfaction which eventually it caused the Patriots, was not to be a home-made dish. The ingredients were those ordinarily used in the best revolutionary kitchens of Paris. They were cooked under the supervision of the most skilled French cooks, and they were tasted by the connoisseurs of the French Directorate, who had promised to savour the dish personally to make it most palatable to the Dutch taste. Then, sizzling-hot from the French fire, it was carried to Holland and was served to the astonished assembly right in the middle of their endless discussions. Why, reader, this appeal to your culinary senses? I want you to stay for the appearance of this famous *râgout à la Directoire*. But it will not be ready before another chapter. If now I hold out hope of a fine dinner to be served after five or six more pages, I can perhaps make you stay through the next chapter, which will be as gloomy as a rainy Sunday in Amsterdam.

IX.

GLORY ABROAD

There was no glory abroad. Naval battles have often been described. Sometimes they are inspiring through the suggestion of superior courage or ability. Frequently they are very dull. Then they belong in a handbook on naval tactics, but not in a popular history. We shall try to make our readers happy by practising the utmost brevity. Paulus was dead, and the new leaders of the navy department were inefficient. They did their best, but private citizens are not changed into successful managers of a navy over night. On paper (patient paper of the eighteenth century, which had contained so many imaginary fleets) there were over sixty Dutch men-of-war. Salaries were officially paid to 17,000 sailors and officers. Of those not more than a score knew their business. The old higher officers were all gone. They were sailing under a Russian flag. They were fighting under the British cross or eking out a penurious half-pay life in little Brunswick, near their old commander-in-chief. As for the sailors, they had had no way of escaping their fate. Poverty had forced them to stay where they were or starve, and they had been obliged to take the new oath of allegiance to support their families. Their quarterdeck now was beautiful with the new legend of Fraternity, Equality, and Liberty painted in big golden letters. Their masts still flew the old glorious flag of red, white, and blue, but now adorned with a gaudy picture of the goddess in whose name war was being waged upon the greater part of the civilized world. At times the men could not stand it. Many a morning it was discovered that the flag had been ruined over night. A hasty knife had cut the divinity out of her corner and had thrown her overboard. But cloth was cheap. A new flag was soon provided, and the goddess of liberty was sewn in once more. To find the culprit was impossible, for upon such occasions the whole fleet was likely to come forward and confess itself guilty. So there the fleet lay, with mutiny averted by the near presence of a French army, and forced to inactivity by the blockade of the British fleet. The admiral of the Dutch squadron was the same Brigadier General de Winter who the year before had tried in vain to reach the ocean. If you look him up in the French biographical dictionary you will find him as Count of Huissen and Marshal of the Empire. In plain Dutch, he was just Jan Willem de Winter and an ardent believer in the most extreme revolutionary doctrines. He had had a little experience at sea, but he had never commanded a ship. Personally brave beyond suspicion, but not in the least prepared for the work which he had been called to do, he had again assumed the command with the cheerfulness with which revolutionary people will undertake any sort of an impossible task. His instructions were secret, or as secret as anything could be which during a number of weeks had been carefully threshed out in all the leading patriotic clubs. The whole plan of this expedition of which Admiral de Winter was to be the head was of that fantastic nature so dearly loved by those who are going to change the world over night. England, of course, the stronghold of all anti-revolutionary forces, was to be the enemy. And, by the way, what a provoking enemy this island proved to be! The churches of the Kremlin could be made into stables for the French cavalry; the domes of Portugal might be turned into pigstys; the palaces of Venice could be used as powder magazines; the storehouses of Holland might be changed into hospitals for French invalids; where French infantry could march or French cavalry could trot, there the influence of France and the ideas of the French could penetrate; but England, with many miles of broad sea for its protection, was the one country which was impregnable. French engineers could do much, but they could not build a bridge across the Channel. French artillery could at times perform wonders of marksmanship, but its guns could not carry across the North Sea. French cavalry had captured a frozen Dutch fleet, but the sea around England never froze. And French infantry, which held the record for long distance marches, could not swim sixty miles of salt water. The fleet, and the fleet alone, could here do the work. At first there had been talk of a concerted action by the French, the Spanish, and the Batavian fleets. But the Patriots would not hear of this plan. Single-handed the Dutch fleet must show that the spirit of de Ruyter and Tromp continued to animate the breasts of all good Batavianites. On the 6th of October, 1797, the fleet sailed proudly away from the roads of Texel. The *Brutus* and the *Equality*, the *Liberty*, the *Batavian*, the *Mars*, the *Jupiter*, the *Ajax*, and the *Vigilant*, twenty-six ships in all, ranging from eighteen to seventy-four cannon, set sail for the English coast. For five days this mythological squadron was kept near the Dutch coast by a western wind. Then it met the British fleet under Admiral Adam Duncan. The British fleet was of equal strength—sixteen ships of the line and ten frigates. But whereas the Batavian fleet was commanded by new officers and manned by disgruntled sailors, the British had the advantage of superior guns, superior marksmanship, better leadership, and a thorough belief in the cause which their country upheld. Off the little village of Camperdown, on the coast of the Department of North Holland, the battle took place. It lasted four hours. After the first fifty minutes the Dutch line had been broken. After the second hour the victory of the British was certain. Two hours more, for the glory of their reputation, the Dutch commanders continued to fight. Vice-Admiral Bloys van Treslong, descendant of the man who conducted the victorious water-beggars to the relief of Leyden in 1574, lost his arm, but continued to defend the *Brutus* until his ship could only be kept afloat by pumping. Captain Hingst of the*Defender* was killed on the bridge. The *Equality* suffered sixty killed and seventy wounded out of a total of one hundred and ninety men. The *Hercules*, set on fire by grapeshot, continued to fight until her commander had been mortally wounded and the flames had reached the powder-house, forcing the men to throw their ammunition overboard. The *Medemblik*, rammed by one of her sister ships, lost fifty men killed and sixty wounded, lost its mast, and was generally shot to pieces before the fight had lasted two hours. And so on through the whole list. Personal bravery could avail little against bad equipment and an indifferent spirit. Ten vessels fell into British hands. One ship, with all its men, perished during the storm which followed the battle. Another one, on the way home, was thrown upon the Dutch coast and was pounded to timber by the waves. All in all, 727 men had been killed and 674 wounded. A few ships, after suffering terribly, reached Dutch harbours.

And for the first time in the history of the Dutch navy, a Dutch admiral was on board a British ship as a prisoner of war.

X.

COUP D'ÉTAT NO. I

Citizen Eykenbroek was in the gin business—an excellent and profitable business which needs close watching, otherwise your workmen will drink the result of their handiwork and all the profits will be lost. Citizen Eykenbroek had not watched. Citizen Eykenbroek had failed. Wherefore, since he had a wife and children, it behooved him to look for another means of livelihood. Citizen Eykenbroek became a speculator in army provisions. Again a profitable business, but not a success as a course in applied ethics. However that be, or perhaps because of all that, Citizen Eykenbroek was the appointed man to act as intermediary between the grumbling Dutch Patriots and the French radicals who held sway in Paris. Armed with credentials given him by the Jacobin Club of Amsterdam, this honourable citizen, with two fellow-conspirators, hastened to Paris.

Since as a speculator in army requisitions he often made the trip to the French capital, his disappearance caused no surprise; and although the Batavian minister in Paris heard of one shabby individual's arrival, he saw no occasion to pay any attention to it. Citizen Eykenbroek, who had not expired when he had told his first lie, did not mind telling a few fibs, and at once he was very successful with the French radicals. His first offer of four hundred thousand good Dutch guilders as a reward for a suitable revolution which would bring all power into the hands of the unionists he gradually increased until it reached the sum of eight hundred thousand. Since no one in Holland had given him the right to offer any monetary reward for the French services, he might easily have made it a few millions. Having paved the way by creating such visions of wealth, Eykenbroek set to work. The great grief of the Dutch Jacobins was the French minister in The Hague. This dignitary, Noel by name, was not in the least a radical. He understood that in this complacent republic little could be gained by decapitational measures, but very much by moderation, the encouragement of trade, the promotion of commerce; and like his friend Cochon, a year or so before, he strongly advised against killing the goose that might again lay so many golden eggs. The Batavian Republic as a thriving commercial commonwealth was a much better asset to the French Republic than the same republic playing a game of revolution, which was very distasteful to the richer classes of the nation. And upon several occasions Noel had firmly reminded his patriotic Dutch friends that, come what may, he would not stand for any works of violence. "Remove Noel," therefore, was one of the most important instructions which Citizen Eykenbroek had taken to Paris upon his memorable voyage. And behold! the promise of half a million in cash at once did its work. The French Directorate suddenly remembered that Citizen Noel had married a Dutch lady. It was not good for France to be represented by a minister who was attached to the republic through such tender bonds of personal affection. Therefore, exit Citizen Noel and his Dutch wife. His successor was a former French minister of foreign affairs. This worthy gentleman, Delacroix by name, cared little for Holland or for its imbecile politics. He regarded his post as a mere stepping-stone to something better (a place in the Directorate perhaps), and fully decided not to interfere in Dutch politics so long as the republic paid its debts and strictly obeyed the orders which were issued from Paris. And since he did not intend to spend too many months in the abominable climate of the low countries, he left Madame Delacroix at home and merely brought his secretary, an individual by the name of Ducagne, who as a spy, a tutor, a newspaper correspondent, and army contractor knew the republic from one end to the other and could help the minister pull the necessary strings. The couple appeared in The Hague during the first part of the year 1797, and their arrival meant that the coast was clear and that the Patriots could go ahead and perform the somersault which was to land the republic upon a pair of unionistic feet. It is an ill defeat which brings nobody any good. The destruction of the Dutch fleet at Camperdown had brought a sudden succour to the unionists. "They had predicted this right along." That most delightful remark, profoundest consolation of all commonplace souls, became their war cry.

"We have predicted this, of federalists, moderates, and all further enemies of union. We will predict the same thing unless we get one country, one treasury, and one navy," and they told their enemies so, black on white. In a document containing nine articles and signed by forty-three of the members of the assembly, more extreme unionists laid down their political beliefs and indicated the remedies through which they proposed to avert another similar disaster. With the exception of parliament, which they wished to consist of only one chamber, but which at the present moment consists of two, their political program contained the fundamentals upon which (with the addition of a King as Executive) the modern Kingdom of the Netherlands is based.

The united patriotic clubs loudly applauded this declaration of unionistic principles. Hisses came from the side of the federalistic villains. Well-intentioned, moderate gentlemen tried to bring about a cessation of all passions. "Citizens, citizens, in the fair name of our great republic, let us go about this matter quietly and deliberately. Let both parties exercise a little more patience. The commission on the constitution is now almost ready. Only six short weeks more and we may expect to hear from it. Just a little more patience."

The French minister was greatly entertained by this little human comedy which he could see enacted in front of his comfortable windows. He made no attempt to hide his superior amusement nor to conceal his profound contempt. Just as in far-off Timbuctoo the French military governor may give broad hints to the native ruler that such and such a thing must be done in such and such a way, so did the French minister upon several occasions at dinners, at his home, and abroad, indicate in the plainest of terms that the assembly must either adopt a constitution after the French pattern or must expect to suffer dire consequences. "This puttering," so his Excellency was pleased to say, "this delaying of vital matters, this keeping of a whole country in suspense for so many years, is really unbearable. If the Hollanders cannot make a constitution for themselves, they had better leave the whole matter to the care of the French."

The assembly, getting knowledge of these rumours (as had been intended by their author), was struck by a sudden wave of patriotism. Unanimously gathered around the imaginary altar of liberty, the members solemnly decided and openly declared that come what may they would save the country or die in the attempt. This sounded very well, but since nobody had asked them to defend or to die, it had little sense. All the country asked was that at last a constitution be adopted and that the government be put upon a regular constitutional basis. That, however, was a different matter, and for the moment the assembly preferred to begin a lengthy debate upon the delicate question whether the anniversary of the decapitation of "Citizen Louis Capet should be celebrated by a public oath of hatred against William of Nassau or not." The unionists said "yes." The federalists said "no." And so they spent a number of days upon this very unprofitable discussion, which ended in a vote which put Citizen Capet and Citizen William both upon the table.

While the assembly was thus agreeably engaged a small number of citizens of a different stamp, but no less interested in the politics of the day, were holding meetings in a little room just around the corner from the assembly. This little group consisted of the secretary of the French embassy, the commander-in-chief of the Batavian army, and a number of the leading unionist members of the assembly. Right under the nose of the dignified assembly, if we may use so colloquial an expression for so wicked a fact, these conspirators were arranging the last details of their little *coup d'état.* The French Directorate had expressed its approval, provided that there was to be no bloodshed. Were the promoters of the plan quite sure that the federalists would offer no armed resistance? Did the triumphant unionist party contemplate violent retribution? "Messieurs," the answer came from The Hague, "compared to your own glorious revolutionists of sainted memory, even the most extreme Dutch Jacobins are like innocent lambs. The little plan which they have originated resembles more a Sunday-school frolic than a real and genuine revolutionary coup."

"All right," Paris reported back, "go ahead and try."

The scene of the dark comedy which we are now about to describe was laid in the old princely courtyard. At two o'clock of a cold winter's night (January 21-22, 1798), a strong detachment of soldiers under command of Daendels occupied the buildings where the assembly met. At four o'clock of the morning the six members of the committee on foreign affairs, under suspicion as aristocrats and enemies of the union, were hauled out of their beds and, shivering, were informed that they must consider themselves under arrest and must not leave their homes. Thereupon they were allowed to go back to bed. At half-after seven the sleepy town opened its curious shutters, noticed that something unusual was in the air, and decided to take a day off. At quarter to eight of the morning, the fifty extreme unionists who were in the plot met at the hotel which had been formerly occupied by the delegates to the Estates from the good town of Haarlem. At eight o'clock sharp their procession started upon its way. Preceded by two cannon, and accompanied and surrounded by trustworthy civil guards and Batavian regulars, the fifty conspirators, the president of the assembly in his official sash at the head of them, walked in state to their meeting hall. At the entrance they were met by General Daendels in full gold lace. Silently the members entered the building, and immediately guards were posted to refuse admission to all those whose names did not appear upon a specially prepared list. The committee on the constitution, however, was allowed to be present in its entirety. At nine o'clock the Speaker of the assembly, Middenrigh by name, in executive session, declared that the country was in danger. ("Hear! hear!") Not an hour was to be lost. (Great excitement.) He appealed to all members to do their full duty to their country. Whereupon the members of the assembly, or such of them as had not been caught by the guard and according to orders had been locked up in the coatroom, arose from their seats and openly avowed their horror of the Stadholdership, of federalism, of anarchy, and of aristocracy. At that moment, however, it was discovered that ten black sheep had strayed into the meeting. They were given the choice between an immediate retraction of their federalist sentiments or leaving the room. They left. At eleven o'clock the executive session was changed into a regular one. The galleries were immediately filled with noisy holiday-makers. The federalist members were released from the coatroom and sadly walked home. They had been informed that from that moment on they had officially ceased to be members of the assembly, that they must not leave The Hague until they were permitted to do so by the military authorities, and that they must not enter into any correspondence with their partisans outside of the city.

At noon the expurgated assembly set to work. It abolished the old rules of the house which for three years had provided a parliamentary procedure which allowed of no practical progress. It abolished all provincial and county sovereignty. And then it took an even more important step, and on the afternoon of the 22d of January, of the year of our Lord 1798, the roaring of many cannon announced to the Batavian people that the republic possessed its first "Constitutional Assembly"—a gathering of true unionists who would not disperse until the constitution of the republic should have become an established fact.

An intermediary body consisting of five members and

presided over by a well-known unionist, Citizen Vreede, was announced to have assumed the executive duties. The assembly approved, and then it appointed a committee of seven to proceed with all haste and make a suitable constitution.

It was now well past the lunch hour, when suddenly there resounded a great applause among the members of the eager galleries.

Enters Citizen Delacroix, minister plenipotentiary and envoy extraordinary from the Republic of France. "Long live the glorious French Republic!" The real author of our little comedy appears to make a curtain speech. He thanked his audience. Really he was greatly touched by such a warm reception. Such energy and such resolution as had been shown that night by the true friends of the fatherland deserved his full approbation. "Continue, Citizens, on this path! The Directory will support you, yea, the whole French nation will applaud you and encourage you on your path toward your high destiny." Loud cheers from the gallery. The Minister sat down.

Then a speech of thanks by the Speaker of the assembly. You can read it if you are so inclined on page 125 of the thirty-fifth volume of Wagenaar, but I have not got the courage to repeat it here. There was a great deal in it about the enemies of liberty, the noble and magnanimous French ally, the peoples of Europe, and the humble desire of the assembly that the Citizen Representative would deign to occupy a seat of honour in this noble hall. And then the Speaker of the house, having obtained permission to leave the chair, descended to the floor of the assembly and among breathless quiet he pressed upon the noble brow of Citizen Delacroix the imprint of a brotherly kiss.

XI.

THE CONSTITUTIONAL

The report of this kiss resounded to Paris. So greatly did it please the French Directorate that they at once increased the number of troops which the republic was obliged to equip and support, and demanded that henceforth the French Government might officially dispose over three fourths of the Batavian army. Let us come down to plain facts. After three years of revolutionary rhetoric the Batavian Republic for all intents and purposes had become a French province—a province inhabited by rather backwoodsy people (the Batavian minister as chief Rube in the Follies of 1798, an enormous success), people who simply never could make up their minds, whose very political upheavals had to be staged abroad, who had to be guided about like small children, and who only received some respect from their neighbours because they still had a few pennies in their pocketbook. But otherwise, Oh lálá! they were so funny! And Citizen Delacroix, having accepted a nice little gratuity (a golden snuffbox studded with diamonds and filled with gold pieces), wrote back to Paris that being minister to The Hague was as good fun as an evening at vaudeville. This, however, was merely the beginning. Much else was to follow soon.

Here we have a country becoming every day more like a French department. And what did the thinking part of the nation do? It continued its petty political quarrels as if it consisted of a lot of villagers engaged in the habitual row in the local vestry. The Orangeistic party of these years reminds us strongly of those pious supporters of the Pope who wish to see the whole kingdom of Italy go to smash in order that his Holiness may return to govern a city which during many previous centuries of his august rule was turned into a byword for civic mismanagement and municipal corruption. The Orangeists sat in their little corner and jeered at everything the patriots did. But they lacked the courage and the conviction to come forward and assist in such constructive work as the revolutionary parties tried to perform.

In previous chapters we have had a chance to talk with considerable irritation about much of what the Patriots did. Do not expect the historian to read through the twenty-three volumes of speeches of the assembly, to study the twelve volumes of Wagenaar containing the history of those three years, to wade through the endless documents addressed to free citizens, and not to feel a personal resentment against his ancestors, who, while the country was in such grave danger, talked and talked and talked without any regard to the threatening facts about them.

It is true that very much can be said in defense of the Patriotic statesmen. They had never enjoyed any political training. For centuries they and their families had been kept out of all governmental institutions. They had not even been allowed to run their own town meeting. There had been no school for parliamentary methods or oratory. And since the death of Paulus they had not possessed a leader of sufficient influence to force one single will upon their ill-organized party. For a moment there was some improvement after the first *coup d'état*. The idea of ending political anarchy by establishing an executive body of five members was a curious one, but it was better than the executive body of more than a hundred which had existed before. And under the spur of the moment the committee on the constitution set to work so eagerly that it finished its labours in as many months as the old assemblies had used years.

The moderate nature of the Dutch people in political matters was again shown after this little upheaval. Two or three clubs and coffee-houses which had shown too open a delight at the former difficulties of the unionists were closed until further notice. A few of the expelled members of the old assembly were temporarily lodged in the house in the woods. But otherwise no enemy of the unionists had to suffer a penalty for his acts or for his words.

The committee of five went to work at once and tried to reëstablish some semblance of order without bothering about political persecutions, and the committee of seven laboured on the new constitution with an ardour which excluded all active participation in such matters as did not pertain to paragraphs and articles and preambles. The French minister energetically assisted them in their task. He had made many a constitution in his own day and knew of what he was talking.

It was a gratifying result that six weeks after the *coup d'état* the committee reported that it was ready to submit the new constitution to the approval of the assembly. On the 6th of March it presented a document consisting of five hundred and twenty-seven articles. Three days sufficed to discuss these articles thoroughly. On the evening of the 17th of March the second constitution of the Batavian Republic was accepted by the entire assembly, and in less than two months after the memorable victory of the unionists the constitution was in such shape that it could be brought before the people.

In the place of the old oligarchic republic it established a centralized government. It provided a strong executive power, which was subject to the will of the legislature. The latter was divided into two chambers, which were to work in cooperation. The final source of all power, however, was brought down to the voters. In all religious and personal matters it tried to furnish complete equality and complete liberty, and as the best means of controlling the legislature and the executive it insisted upon absolute freedom for the political press.

In the matter of finances the country henceforward would be a union and not a combination of seven contrary-minded pecuniary interests. The provinces, divided according to a new system, retained such local government as was necessary for the proper conduct of their immediate business, but in all matters of any importance the provinces became subject to the higher central powers in The Hague.

Finally it brought about one great improvement for which many men during many centuries had worked in vain. It established a cabinet. Eight agents (we would call them ministers) would henceforth handle the general departments of the government. In this way, in the year of grace 1798, disappeared that endless labyrinth of committees and sub-committees and sub-sub-committees within sub-committees in which during former centuries all useful legislation had lost its way and had miserably perished.

This time when the constitution was brought before the people the result was very different from that of the year before. Of those who took the trouble to walk to the polls, twelve out of every thirteen declared themselves in favour of the new constitution. On the 1st of May, 1798, the constitutional assembly was informed that the Batavian people had, by an overwhelming majority, accepted the constitution, and that its fruitful labours were over. The Batavian republic now was a bona-fide modern state and all was well with the world.

XII.

COUP D'ÉTAT NO. II

Who was the wise man who first said that a little power was a dangerous thing? Oh, Citizen Vreede, who knew more about the price and quality of cloth than of politics; Brother van Langen, who so dearly loved the little glory and the fine parties to which his exalted rank as one of the five members of the executive gave him admission; Rev. Mr. Fynje, who once used to fill the devout Baptist eye with pious tears and who now talked for the benefit of the Jacobin gallery—why did ye not disappear from our little stage when your rôle was over, when the curtain dropped upon the constitution which you had just given to an expectant fatherland? It would have been so much better for your own reputation. It would have been so much better for the reputation of the good cause which you had so well defended. It would have been so much better for the country which, at one time, you loved so well.

For listen what happened: In an evil hour the constitutional assembly, under pressure of its aforementioned leaders, declared itself to be the representative assembly provided for by their own constitution, and calmly parcelled out the seats of the upper and the lower chambers among its own members. At the same time the intermediary executive of five members was declared to be a permanent body. And of the entire constitutional assembly only six members had the courage to declare themselves openly against this grab, whereupon they were promptly removed from the meeting by the others. Indeed this was a very stupid thing to do. For it gave all the enemies of union a most welcome chance to attack the unconstitutional procedure of those who had just made this self-same constitution, the rules of which they now violated. It gave them a chance to talk about graft and to insinuate that not love for the country but love for the twelve thousand a year actuated the five directors when they staged this unlawful affair. It exploded all the noble talk of an unselfish love for a united fatherland when at the very first chance the unionists disregarded their own laws and continued a situation by which they personally were directly profited.

Furthermore, the glory of their sudden elevation went disastrously to the heads of several of the men who had played a leading rôle during the fight against the federalists. It did not take a long time to show the unionists that their constitution, while theoretically a perfect success, did not bring all the practical results which had been hoped for. A country which has been running in a provincial groove for more than three centuries cannot suddenly forget all its antecedents and become a well-organized, centralized state. The old officials who had to be retained until new ones could be trained for these duties were trained to perform their duties in a certain old-fashioned way. The constitution asked them to do their new work in a very different way. The result was confusion and congestion. The directors and the new secretaries of the different departments worked with great industry. Their desks, however, were loaded with new labours. All the thousand and one little items which formerly had been decided in the nearest village or town now had to be referred to The Hague. And soon it became clear that the constitution was too good, that it had centralized too much, and that all its energy marred what it tried to do to such an extent that now nothing at all was ever accomplished.

The leaders of the unionist party, especially the more ardent of the Patriots (for although the name began to disappear the party and its ideals continued), began to suspect bad faith among their opponents. The chaotic condition of internal affairs, according to them, was due to the machinations of their federalist and

Orangeist opponents. And they began to lose their heads. They wanted to show their power and make clear to their enemies that they were not afraid. First of all, they placed the federalist members who were still detained in the house in the woods under very strict supervision and talked of weird plots of the country's enemies, and dismissed all the ancient clerks who on account of their slowness were suspected of Orangeistic inclination, and ended by building a foolish temple of liberty on an open place in The Hague, where they wasted much bad rhetoric and told the astonished populace that they, the unionists, would stop at nothing if it came to a defence of what they considered their most holy rights. But when they came to this point the sun of French approbation began to hide itself behind dark clouds of disapproval, and a threatening thunder of discontent began to rumble in far-off Paris.

And now we come to an amusing episode which better than any lengthy disquisition shows the rapidity with which France was changing from her stormy revolutionary nature to a well-established and well-regulated nation of respectable citizens. A year before Delacroix had been sent to the republic to supplant a French minister who no longer seemed to be the right man in the right place. And now M. Talleyrand, the estimable French minister of foreign affairs, did not feel that Delacroix fully represented the sentiments of the Directorate, and decided to get rid of him and fill his place with a more suitable personage. As a preliminary measure he sent to The Hague a certain Champigny-Aubin, whose express duty it was to spy on Delacroix, and who was to get into touch with the defeated federalist party, while his chief supported the unionists. For several weeks an entertaining situation followed. Delacroix played with the radicals; Aubin played with the conservatives. Now it so happened that among those who were discontented for one reason or another there was that stormy petrel, General Daendels. He had acted an important rôle during the first *coup d'état*, but when it was over he had found the commandership in chief of the Batavian forces, momentarily placed into the hands of the French commander, had not been returned to himself. He did not fancy this rôle of second fiddle at all and became an enemy of the Dutch directors and the unionistic party. And one fine morning the directors were informed that their general had left without asking their permission and that he had been last seen moving rapidly in the direction of Paris. Now the directors ought to have taken this hint. They knew all about conspiracies from their own recent experiences, and they should have surmised that Daendels did not trot to Paris to take in the sights of that interesting city. But, on the other hand, did they not daily meet and confer with his Excellency the French minister? Was not Delacroix their sworn friend and did not the French army support him in his affection for the present Batavian Government? Yes, indeed. But the directors could not know that the home government had secretly disavowed their diplomatic representative and only waited for a suitable occasion to recall him.

Well, General Daendels safely reached Paris and saw the French directors. After a few days a request came from The Hague for his arrest as a deserter. The directors deposited this request in the official waste-paper basket and quietly finished their arrangements with the Batavian general; and when, after a few days, he returned to The Hague, all the details for the second *coup d'état* had been carefully discussed and all plans had been made.

Daendels came back just in time to be the guest of honour at a large dinner which was given by a number of private gentlemen who called themselves "Friends of the Constitution." At this banquet he appeared in his habitual rôle of conquering hero, and was the subject of tipsy ovations. Indeed, so great was the racket of this patriotic party that the directors who lived nearby could distinctly hear the unholy rumour of these festivities. And since, for the matter of discipline, it is not good that a general who has left his post without official leave shall upon his return be made the subject of a great popular demonstration, they decided that the next morning the general and the leaders of this dinner should be put under arrest. *Dis aliter visum.* The very same day upon which Daendels should have been put into jail, while the directors were eating their dinner in company with the French minister, who should enter but General Daendels and a couple of his grenadiers. General commotion. Tables and chairs were overturned, dishes were thrown to the floor, and much excellent wine was spilled. A couple of the directors jumped out of a window and landed in the flowerbeds of the garden. But the garden was surrounded by more soldiers and the escaping directors were captured and put under arrest. The others, not wishing to risk their limbs, appealed to the French minister. But the minister was unceremoniously told to hold his tongue and mind his own business. He was then conducted through the door and deposited in the street. Two of the directors who had escaped during the first commotion hid themselves in the attic of the building. There they stayed until all searching parties had failed to discover them, and then managed to make their escape through a back door.

This violent attack upon the inviolable directors was but one part of Daendels' program. At the head of his troops he now hastened to the assembly. The upper chamber had already adjourned for the day, but in the lower chamber the Speaker defied the invading soldiers from his chair and started to make a speech. Two of the soldiers took him by the arms, and the chair was vacated. A number of members, led by Citizen Middenrigh, the same who two months before had conducted that unionist procession which dissolved the constitutional assembly of the federalist majority, heroically defied the soldiers and flatly refused to leave. No violence was used, but a guard was placed in front of the entrance and the assembly was left in darkness to talk and argue and harangue as much as it desired. Tired and hungry, the disgusted members gave up fighting the inevitable and slowly left the hall. Two dozen of the more prominent unionists were arrested, and quiet settled down once more upon the troubled city.

The prisoners were conducted to the house in the woods, and that famous edifice upon this memorable evening resembled one of those absurd clubs which American cartoonists delight to create and to fill with members of their own fancy. For the federalist victims of the 23rd of January and the unionist victims of the 12th of June sat close at the same table, and as fellow-jailbirds they partook of the same prison food and slept under the same roof.

At nine o'clock the second *coup d'état* was over and everybody went to bed. In this way ended the most violent day of the Dutch struggle for constitutional government.

What would Mr. Carlyle have done with a revolution like that?

XIII.

CONSTITUTION NO. II AT WORK

The election which took place in June of the year 1798 brought an entirely new set of men into the assembly. The voters, tiring of experiments which invariably seemed to end in disaster and a parade of Daendels at the head of a number of conspiring gentlemen, elected a number of men of whom little could be said but that they were "sound" and not given over to the dreaming of impracticable visions. They could be trusted to run the government in a peaceful way, they would undoubtedly try to reëstablish credit, and they would give the average citizen a chance to pursue his daily vocation without being bothered with eternal elections.

In the two chambers which convened on the 31st of July of the same year the moderates, who had left the first assembly in disgust, were represented by a large majority. A well-known gentleman of very moderate views was elected to the chair and everybody set to work. First of all, the assembly had to consider what ought to be done with the members of the old assemblies who as prisoners of state were running up an enormous bill for board and lodging in the comfortable house in the woods. The French directors in Paris dropped the hint that it might be well to let bygones be bygones and release the prisoners. The doors of the prison were accordingly opened, the prisoners made their little bow, and left the stage. A good deal of their work liveth after them. We thank them for their kind services, but the play will be continued by more experienced actors.

When this difficulty had thus been settled in a very simple

way the assembly was called upon to appoint five new directors. Here was a difficult problem. The old, experienced politicians sulked on their Sabine farms. And, terrible confession to make, the younger politicians had not yet reached the two-score years which was demanded by the constitution of those who aspired to serve their country as its highest executives. Finally, however, five very worthy gentlemen were elected. None of them has left a reputation as either very good or very bad. Under the circumstances that was exactly what the country most needed.

The new assembly and the new directors went most conscientiously about their duties. They promptly suppressed all attempts at reaction within the chambers and without. They kept the discussions on the narrow path between Orangeism, federalism, anarchy, and aristocracy, and for the next three years they made an honest attempt to promote the new order of things to the best of their patient ability and with scrupulous obedience to the provisions of the constitution. According to the law, one of the five directors had to resign each year. These changes occurred without any undue excitement. The sort of men that came to take the vacant places were of the same stamp as their predecessors. As assistant secretaries of some department of public business or as judges of a provincial court they would have been without a rival; but they hardly came up to the qualities of mind and character required of men able to save the poor republic from that perdition toward which the gods were so evidently guiding her.

XIV.

MORE GLORY ABROAD

While we have been watching our little domestic puppet show and have seen how the figures were being moved by the dextrous fingers of some hidden French performer, what has been happening upon the large stage of the world? Great and wonderful things have happened. A little half-pay lieutenant, of humble parentage, bad manners, ungrammatical language, but inordinate ambition, has hewn his way upward until as commander-in-chief of the French armies he has made all the land surrounding the country of his adoption into little tributary republics, has obliged the Sphinx to listen to his oratory, and has caused his frightened enemies to forget their mutual dislike to such an extent that they combine into the second coalition of England, Prussia, Russia, and Turkey. The Batavian Republic, bound to France by her defensive and offensive treaty, found herself suddenly in war with the greater part of the European continent. Now if there was anything which the new assembly of moderates did not wish, it was another outbreak of hostilities.

Once more a strong British fleet was blockading the Dutch coast. The Dutch fleet, bottled up in the harbour of Texel, was again doomed to inactivity. As for the army, it was supposed to consist of 20,000 men, but the majority of the soldiers were raw and untrained recruits and useless for immediate action upon any field of battle.

Often during the previous years the French had contemplated an invasion of the British Isles. This game of invasion is one which two people can play. And on the 27th of August, 1799, the directors, who were patiently working their way through the mountains of official red tape demanded by the over-centralized Batavian Government, were informed by courier from Helder that a large hostile fleet had been sighted near the Dutch coast. Frantic orders were given to Daendels to take his army and prepare for defense. But the general, in no mild temper, reported that he had neither "clothes for his men, nor horses for his cavalry, nor straw for his horses." And before he had obtained the money with which to buy part of these necessaries the British fleet had captured the Dutch one and had thrown 15,000 men, English and Russian, upon the Dutch coast. A week later these were followed by more men, until half a hundred thousand foreign soldiers were upon the territory of the Batavian Republic and within two days' march from Amsterdam.

Daendels, with such men as he could muster, bravely marched to the front, and from behind dikes and in the narrow streets of ancient villages opened a guerilla warfare upon the invaders. French troops were reported to be on their way to help the Batavians, but could not arrive before a couple of days. The country was in a dangerous position, and yet the British-Russian invasion petered out completely, and, full of promise, was changed into a complete failure.

This was due partly to the dilatoriness of the English commander and to the bad understanding between Englishman and Russian. But worst of all, the allies, for the second time, committed the blunder which had cost them so dearly just before the battle of Verdun. The young Prince of Orange had joined this expedition, and some enthusiast (if not he himself) had thought to improve the occasion by the issuing of a high-sounding proclamation.

This document treated the entire revolution as so much personal wickedness, as the machinations of vicious and ambitious people who desired to change the country's government merely for the benefit of their own pockets. It called upon all fatherlanders to drive the French usurpers out and to return to their old allegiance to what the proclamation was pleased to call their "sovereign ruler."

De landing der Engelschen. Invasion of the British

This sovereign ruler was none less than old William V. But if there was anything which the people as a whole did not desire, it was a return to the days of that now forgotten Stadholder. Federalists and unionists were bad enough, but the comparative liberty of the present moment was too agreeable to make the citizens desire a repetition of those old times when all the voters and assemblymen of the present hour were merely silent actors in a drama which was not of their making and not of their approval. And with quite rare unanimity the Batavians rejected this proclamation of their loving Stadholder and made ready to defend the country against the invader who came under the guise of a deliverer.

The hereditary Prince settled down in the little town of Alkmaar of famous memory and waited. He waited a week, but nothing happened except that the troops of the allies, badly provisioned by their commissary departments, began to steal and plunder among the Dutch farmers. And when another week had passed it had become manifestly clear that the Prince and his army could not count upon the smallest support from the Batavians. By that time, too, the French army had been greatly strengthened. Commanded by the French Jacobin Brune, who loved a fight as well as he did brandy, the defences of the republic were speedily put into excellent shape. Krayenhoff, our friend of the revolution of Amsterdam, now a very capable brigadier general of engineers, inundated the country around Amsterdam, while the English, under their slow and ponderous commander Yorke, were still debating as to the best ways and means of attack. When finally the allies went over to that attack they found themselves with the sea behind them, with sand dunes and impassable swamps on both sides, and with a strong French and a smaller Batavian army in front of them. And when they tried to drive this army out of its position they were badly defeated in a number of small fights; and a month after they had marched from Helder to Alkmaar they marched back from Alkmaar to Helder, shipped their enormous number of sick and wounded on board the fleet, and departed, cursing a country where even the drinking water had to be transported across the North Sea, where it always rained, and where, even if it did not rain, the water sprang from the soil and turned camps and hospitals and trenches into uninhabitable puddles.

Dutch troops rushing to the defence of the coast

The Batavian army was proud of itself and was praised by others. The men had stood the test of the war much better than people had dared to hope.

But what good, apart from a little glory, had all their bravery done them? On land they had beaten the English, but in far-away Asia the British fleet had taken one Dutch colony after the other, until of the large colonial empire there remained but the little island of Decima, in Japan. Upon a strip of territory of a few hundred square feet the old red, white, and blue flag of Holland continued to fly. Everywhere else it had been hauled down.

XV.

CONSTITUTION NO. III

On the 9th of November, 1799, Citizen Bonaparte, the successful commander-in-chief of the armies of the Directorate of France, decided that his employers had done enough talking and that the time had come to send them about their business. The Jacobin rabble in the street protested. Citizen Bonaparte put up two cannon. The rabble jeered at his toy guns. Citizen Bonaparte fired. The rabble fled whence it came. The next day the legislative body was summarily dismissed. The French Revolution was over.

Biologically speaking, Citizen Bonaparte was the second son of Madame Laetitia Bonaparte, née Ramolino, the wife of a Corsican lawyer of some small local importance. His spiritual mother, however, sat on the Place de la Concorde, knitted worsted stockings, and counted the heads which the guillotine chopped off. When his day of glory came, Bonaparte did not forget his faithful mother, and surrounded her with his signs of love and affection. But the foster-mother who had helped him directly to his glory, without whom he never might have been anything but the husband of the attractive Madame Josephine, he neglected, and when she seemed to stand between him and his success he dispatched her into the desert of oblivion, a region which during revolutionary times is never very far distant from the scene of momentary action.

What Napoleon Bonaparte knew about Holland cannot have been very much. Geography, in a general sense, was not his strong point. Like everybody else in Paris, he must have known something about the Batavian Republic, and, like everybody else, he must have received vague notions of the dilatory methods, the insignificant acts, and the clumsiness of the different Batavian missions which sporadically appeared in Paris. Ginstokers who prepared parliamentary revolutions as delegates from private political clubs, generals who left their posts and went trotting to Paris to arrange another upheaval in the assembly of their native country, were not the type of men in whom the future emperor delighted.

Of any sentiment or liking for the Dutch trait and character we find no vestige in Napoleon. There were one or two Dutch generals who won his favour, and one admiral even gained his friendship. He appreciated Dutch engineers because they could build good fortifications and excellent pontoon bridges. In general, however, the slow and deliberate Hollander greatly annoyed the man of impulsive deeds, and the tenacity with which these futile people defended their petty little rights and prerogatives, when actual and immense honours were in store for all men with devotion and energy, filled Napoleon with an irritation and a contempt which he never tried to conceal.

The French Dictator felt but one interest in the Dutch Republic—a material one. In the first place, he wanted the Dutch gold to use for his expeditions against all his near and distant neighbours. In the second place, he contemplated using the strategic position of the republic in his great war upon the British Kingdom. And as soon as he had been elected First Consul he approached the republic with demands for loans and voluntary donations, which were both flatly refused. The Amsterdam bankers were not willing to consider any French loan just then, and the Dutch assembly declared that it could not produce the 50,000,000 guilders which the Consul wanted. It was simply impossible. The Consul retaliated by a very strict enforcement of the terms of the French treaty by which the republic was bound to equip and maintain 25,000 French soldiers. This, in turn, so greatly increased the expenses of the republic that many citizens paid more than half of their income in taxes. It was indeed a very unfortunate moment for such an experiment. The second constitution was by no means a success. Of the many promised reorganizations of the internal government not a single one had as yet been instituted. The reform of the financial system existed on paper but had not yet come nearer to realization than had the proposed reorganization of the militia. The new system of legal procedure was still untried, and the new national courts had not yet been established. The codification of civil and penal law had not yet been begun. Public instruction was under a minister of its own, but it remained as primitive as ever before. The reform of the municipal government had not yet been attempted. The central government of the different departments had been put into somewhat better shape than before, but everything about it was still in the first stages of development. The constitution which had promised to be all things to all men was nothing to any one. The system of government which it provided was too complicated. It looked as if there must be a third change in the management of the Batavian Republic. General Bonaparte was asked for his opinion. General Bonaparte at that moment was going through one of the sporadic changes in his nature. He began to have his hair cut and pay attention to the state of his linen. He commenced to understand that a revolution might be all very well, but that a firm and stable government had enormous advantages. And if the rich people in Holland wished to drop some of their former revolutionary notions and make their government more conservative, they certainly were welcome to the change.

This time there was not even a *coup d'état*. The legislative assembly—the combined meeting of both houses—convened solemnly, like a house of bishops, and proposed a revision of the constitution.

On the 16th of March, 1801, a committee was appointed to draw up a more practical constitution, one more in accord with the historical development of the people. The committee went to work with eagerness, and with the French ambassador as their constant adviser. General Bonaparte was kept informed of all the proceedings, and everything went along as nicely as could be desired. But when the work was done the legislative assembly, after a very complicated discussion, suddenly rejected the new constitution five to one.

What the assembly could not do, the Dutch directors could do. Yes, but the difficulty was that two of the five directors seemed to be against revision. "Three directors are better than five," came back from Paris. The two opposing directors were informed that their opinion would no longer be asked for, and the three others hired a second-class newspaper man who had seen better days and ordered him to draw up a new constitution. Our distinguished colleague, who used to make a living writing political speeches for the members of the different assemblies, set to work to earn his extra pennies, and in less than the time which had been allowed him, his constitution, neatly copied, was in the hands of the three directors. They sent it to Paris. Napoleon changed a few minor articles, but approved of the document as a whole. Now, according to the rules of the old constitution, the document should have been sent to the members of the assembly for their approval. The directors, however, did not bother about such small details, and had the constitution printed and sent directly to the voters. The two discarded directors and the assembly protested. But this time there was not even a chance for defiance or for a heroic stand in parliament. The doors of the assembly were locked and were kept locked. The assemblymen could protest in the street, but for all practical purposes they had ceased to exist.

On the 1st of October, 1801, the vote of the people was taken. It appeared that there were five times as many nays as yeas. Therefore the nays had it?

Not while Consul Bonaparte resides in the Tuilleries.

How many voters were there in the republic? 416,419.

How many had voted in all? 68,990.

Well, count all those who did not vote among the yeas and see how the sum will come out then? A very ingenious method. The count was made, and then the yeas had it.

XVI.

THE THIRD CONSTITUTION AT WORK

He new constitution was reduced to only 106 articles. The sovereign people, with all due respect for their votes, were deprived of most of their former power. The chief executive and legislative power was vested in a body of twelve men. They were appointed by the different provinces, which were reëstablished in their old form, with their old borders, and with most of their former local sovereignty. The two chambers were reduced to one legislative body of thirty-five members. It had the power of veto over the laws proposed by the executive, but could not originate laws nor propose changes. The individual ministers were abolished, but a cabinet was formed out of a council of many members, from three to six for each department. There was to be municipal autonomy. All religious denominations regained those possessions which they had had at the beginning of the revolution of 1795. All other matters of government, the exact form and mode of voting, and such other insignificant details were left to some future date when the executive would decide upon them.

On the same day, when the absent votes of the Batavian Republic saved the third constitution, the preliminaries of the peace between France and England were signed. After seven years of stagnation, the ocean once more was open to Dutch ships, and Dutch commerce once more could visit the furthermost corners of the globe.

The country again could go to work.

Armed bark of the year 1801

XVII.

ECONOMIC CONDITION

Here was a splendid dream of a rejuvenated country eagerly striving to regain its lost importance. But a milkman who comes around once in every seven years will lose his customers. And the Dutch trader, who as the common carrier and the middleman had been for many centuries as regular in the performances of his duties as the useful baker and butcher and grocer of our own domestic acquaintance, found when he came back after half a dozen years that his customers, tired of waiting for him, had gone for their daily needs to a rival and did not contemplate a return to a tradesman who had neglected them during so many years. And when the ships which for seven years had been rotting in the harbours had been sufficiently repaired to venture forth upon the seas, and when they had gathered a cargo of sorts, there was no one to whom they could go to sell their wares.

In the fall of the Dutch Republic we have tried to describe how, gradually, the Hollander lost his markets. This chapter upon our economic condition during the Batavian Republic can be very short. We shall have to describe how, driven out of the legitimate trade, the Dutch shipper entered the wide field of illegitimate business enterprises until at last he disappeared entirely from a field of endeavour in which honesty is not only the best policy but is also the only policy which sooner or later does not lead to ruin. The large commercial houses, of course, could stand several years of depression, but the smaller fry, the humbler brethren who had always kept themselves going on a little floating capital, these were soon obliged either to go out of existence altogether or to enter upon some illicit affair. Quite naturally they chose the latter course, and soon they found themselves in that vast borderland of commerce where honesty merely consists in not being found out.

The Executive Council of the East India Company

At first they traded under neutral flags and with neutral papers. But the British during the prolonged war with France did not stick too closely to international law, and every ship that was under suspicion of not being a bona-fide foreign ship, but a Dutch ship under disguise, was confiscated, taken to England, and there publicly sold. Every variation upon the wide subject of fake papers, fake passports, and counterfeit sailing-orders was tried, but invariably these ingenious schemes were discovered by the British policemen who controlled the high seas, and finally this commerce had to be given up entirely as being too risky.

Then all sorts of even more wonderful plans were developed by the diligent Dutch traders. Here is a scheme at once so brilliant and so simple that we must relate it:

Messrs. A. and B., honourable merchants from Amsterdam, enter into a partnership. A. goes to London and as an Englishman enters business. B. stays at home. A. equips a privateer. B. loads a ship and gets as much insurance as he possibly can. The ship of B. leaves the Dutch harbour and is captured by the ship of A. It is taken to England and ship and cargo are publicly sold. A. gets the profits of his buccaneering expedition. B. collects the insurance. The partners have in this way made twice the amount of their original investment, minus the insignificant loss on the ship. At the end of the year the two merchants divide the spoils and both get rich. This method had the disadvantage of being too easy. A deadly competition set in. Finally the insurance companies discovered the swindle and refused to insure. That stopped the business.

From that moment on the only way of doing business across the water was to take the risk of capture, to try to run the blockade of the British fleet in the North Seas and reach some safe foreign port. When the year 1801 came hardly a dozen ships which flew the Dutch flag dared to cross the ocean. Not a single whaler was seen off the coast of Greenland; the Dutch fishermen had deserted the North Sea; the channel was closed to Dutch trade; the Mediterranean, where once Dutch had been a commonly understood language, did not see any Dutch ships for many years; the Baltic, the scene of the first Dutch commercial triumphs, no longer witnessed the appearance of the Dutch grain carrier who during so many centuries had provided the daily bread for millions of people. This disappearance of the commercial fleet meant the absolute ruin of many industries which up to that time had been kept alive by such demand as there was for planed wood, nets, rope, tar, and the countless things which went into the making of the old sailing-ship. The eighteenth century had been a bad period for these industries.

The beginning nineteenth century killed them. The great manufacturing centres like Leiden and Haarlem became the famous *villes mortes* about which we like to read, but in which we do not care to live. Hollow streets, grass growing between the cobblestones, a few old families slowly dwindling away and using up the funds of former generations; a population ill fed and badly housed, physically degenerating and morally perishing under the load of philanthropy by which it was kept alive; the whole life of the city, once exuberant and open, retiring to the back room where the sinful world cannot be seen; where, around the family tea table, and with the patriarchal pipe, dull resignation is found in that same Bible which once, and not so many years before, had inspired their ancestors to a display of vitality and of energetic enterprise which has been unsurpassed in European history. All optimism gone to make place for a leaden despondency and a feeling that no attempt of the individual can avail against the higher decrees of a cruel Providence. It is a terrible picture. It remained true for almost three generations. Let us be grateful that we in our own day have seen the last of it.

THE RISE OF THE DUTCH KINGDOM

Dutch ships frozen in the ice

In the colonies, as has been said before, the same state of ruin existed as at home. The West India Company had been bankrupt for almost a score of years. The colonies in South America, the rich sugar plantations for which once we sacrificed the unprofitable harbour of New York, were in the year 1801 being worked for the benefit of the British conqueror. Holland had lost them and had lost their profits. In the year 1798, by article 247 of the first constitution, the East India Company had been suspended. This enormous commercial institution, which with a minimum of effort had produced a maximum of results, went out of existence like a candle. Her loss was a terrible blow to Amsterdam. During the last years, when the affairs of the company were going from bad to worse, many loans had been taken up to meet the current expenses. Amsterdam, which had the greatest interest in hiding the actual condition of the company, had invariably provided these loans. Its City Bank still had an inexhaustible supply of cash, but with her trade in foreign securities ruined by the long wars, and her trade in domestic securities destroyed by the demise of Dutch manufacturing and Dutch shipping, with the enormous international banking business made impossible by the unsettled conditions of the revolutionary wars, the bank could only be maintained by very doubtful financial expedients. And when this pillar of Dutch society began to tremble upon its foundations, which were no longer sound, what was to become of the Dutch banks?

Failures of large commercial houses became disastrously frequent. Each failure in turn affected larger circles of business institutions. Even the expedient of using some of the ancestral capital became difficult where there was no market for the securities which the people wished to sell. Dividends upon foreign securities were passed year after year; taxes went up higher every six months. Such a long siege upon its prosperity no country could stand. And while the people were thus being impoverished, what did the government and what did the French allies do to bring about some improvement? France did nothing at all. The Dutch Government sometimes sent a mild protest to London and asked the British Government not to confiscate ships under a neutral flag, protestations which of course remained unanswered.

Here is another little sum in arithmetic which will explain more than a lengthy disputation upon the subject of our national ruin. It is a list of the current expenses and revenues for a number of years:

	GUILDERS
In 1795 the expenses were	51,000,000
Revenue	17,000,000
Deficit	34,000,000

In 1796 expenses and revenue were the same.

In 1797 the expenses were	42,000,000
Revenue	20,000,000
Deficit	22,000,000

In 1798 the expenses were	31,000,000
Revenue	21,000,000
Deficit	10,000,000

But when in 1799 the English and Russians invaded the country and the revenues were appropriated according to the new style provided, the expenses were 80,000,000, the revenue was 36,000,000, and the deficit was 44,000,000. And these deficits, year after year, had to be covered by extra loans, until at last a heavy loan was carried to pay the dividends upon the original loan. Even with the three billions which the republic was reported to have gathered during former centuries, there is but one possible end to such a system of finance: That end is called national bankruptcy.

Batavia—The fashionable quarter

A country place

XVIII.

SOCIAL LIFE

Whether man is merely a chemical compound driven by economic energies or something higher and more sublime is a question which from the inexperience of our youth we dare not decide. But that something in human society is apt to go wrong the moment the *homo sapiens* leaves the straight path between the economic too much and too little is a truth which we are willing to defend against all comers. The trouble during revolutionary times is that the well-worn, old-fashioned, narrow road is no longer visible. The old beacons of proper conduct have been removed, new ones have not yet been provided, and people wander hither and thither, and tumble from one extreme into the other.

In the Batavian Republic in 1795, as the Dutch expression has it, the locks were opened wide. Everybody could do what he pleased. The old rules of polite society were discarded. Batavians were no longer to be slaves neither to certain prescribed masters nor of certain well-defined manners. Of course when almost two million people, rigidly divided into innumerable classes, are suddenly transformed into so many equal citizens, a terrible social cataclysm must take place. During the joyful hysteria of the first few months this was not noticed. The people seemed to forget that all social questions are the result of historical compromises and have a historical growth—that they are not allowed to exist for the benefit of a single class of citizens. A Batavian Republic without titles and official ranks, without coats-of-arms and distinguishing uniforms, was no doubt very desirable and very noble and very highly humane. But the change was too sudden and too abrupt, and in the end it did an enormous amount of harm.

Skating on the river Maas at Rotterdam

During the fifty years that had gone before, the patriotic press had shrieked contumelies upon the regents, who had refused to commit political suicide for a class which they, however, considered to be their inferiors. In this fight all good manners had finally disappeared. It had become a guerilla warfare of violent pamphlets—a muddy battle of mutual vituperation. The regents, however, although a degenerating class, had maintained until the very end a certain ideal of personal manners which had set a standard for all classes. The political upheaval of 1795 brought a number of men to the front who did not possess these outward advantages of a polished demeanour, and therefore despised them. According to them, the country needed men of pure principles (their principles) and not men who could merely bow and scrape. Any intelligent man could hold an office provided he was sound in doctrine (their doctrine). With the ideal of a cultivated man violently thrown out of the community the standard of the schools had at once suffered. It was no longer necessary to possess a general education to be eligible for a higher position. As a result, the universities had not been able to insist upon the old high standards, and when the universities weakened in their demands the other schools had immediately followed suit. This disintegration soon made itself apparent in all sorts of ways. Why write good books or good poetry when the people asked for and were contented with the cheaper variety? Why keep up an artistic ideal when the people wanted vulgar and cheap prints? The few good novelists of the eighteenth century were no longer read. Their place was taken by a number of scribblers, who, by flattering the commonest preferences and by appealing to the worst taste of the large army of voters, made themselves rich and their books popular. They gave the public what it liked. And the public thought them very famous men indeed. It was the same thing in art. We cannot remember ever having seen or ever having heard any one who had ever seen a single good picture painted during the Batavian days. The prints which commemorated the current events are so bad as to be altogether hopeless.

The sovereign people were flattered with a persistency and a lack of delicacy which would have incensed even the worst and most astute of tyrants. The masses, however, did not notice it, and bought the complimentary pictures with great pride in their own virtue. Posterity has thought differently about it, and whereas the prints of the seventeenth and the eighteenth centuries are carefully collected, the prints of the Batavian Republic are usually left as food to the industrious domestic mouse.

But aside from these merely ideal considerations (for a nation may be great and prosperous and yet lack entirely in artistic perception) the ordinary daily life of the community suffered a worse blow than it experienced through the loss of the colonies. During the old commercial days there had been a great many slippery customers who had managed to make their living in very questionable ways. On the whole, however, the leading merchants had maintained a fairly high standard of commercial integrity from which no one dared to avert too openly. Now, in the year 1795, all this changed. The new men were not bound to these iron rules of conduct. A good many of the old unwritten rules and regulations of trade were thrown overboard as being antiquated. Army contractors and questionable speculators entered into the field of Dutch politics and introduced the dangerous standards of people who have managed to get rich overnight. Nobody likes to see his neighbour eating a better dinner than he can afford himself. If a purveyor of army shoes could suddenly keep a carriage and pair and yet be respected by the men with whom he associated, why, the people asked, should we criticise his methods? He is not punished by social contempt. He is treated with great respect because he can entertain in such a very handsome way. And soon the young boy next door tried the same trick of speculation and began to feel a deep contempt for the old-fashioned and slow ways of his immediate ancestors.

THE RISE OF THE DUTCH KINGDOM

Trades

The better element of the community in the general disorganization which followed the revolution found itself deserted, laughed at for its high standards, looked at with the pathetic interest which enterprising young men feel for old fogies who are behind the times. "The poor old people simply would not look facts in the face. Why insist on living in Utopia? Utopia was such a very dreary place." Until, finally, these excellent people either succumbed, which was very rare, or retired from active life, and within the circle of their own home waited for better days and more ideal times. And the general tone of Batavian society was indicated by a class to whom riches meant an indulgence in all the material things of which they had dreamed during their former days of poverty. Easy come, easy go—in money matters as well as in morals. The new class of rich people, living without any restraint, followed its own inclinations, but obeyed no set rules of conduct. The sudden influx of ten thousand French officers, and Heaven knows how many foreign soldiers, also brought a dangerous element into a single community.

It is true that the discipline of the French soldiers had been exemplary, but the men trained in the happy-go-lucky school of the Paris which had followed the puritanical days of the sainted Maximilian Robespierre did not assist in establishing a deeper respect for good morals. The old days of parsimonious living and respect for one's betters were gone forever. Under the new dispensation no one was anybody else's better, and everybody lived as well as his purse or his credit allowed him to.

During the first years of the republic a number of men had suddenly grown rich. These vulgar personages threw their money out of the windows in the form of empty champagne bottles. Outside of their house of mirth a motley congregation of hungry people hovered. They drank what was left in the discarded bottles; they feasted on the remains of the uneaten pastry; they dreamed of the golden days when luck should turn and they should be inside with the worshippers of the fleshpots. The best part of the nation, however, disgusted with these vulgar doings, retired from all active life. It preferred a dull existence of simple honesty to a roisterous feast on the brink of a moral and financial abyss. And quietly the good people waited for the great change that was certain to come, when the nation once more should return to a sound mode of living, and when the resplendent adventurers of the moment should have been relegated back into that obscurity from which they never ought to have emerged.

XIX.

PEACE

What can we say of the next five years—of the five years during which the Batavian Republic lived under her third constitution and outwardly exercised all the functions of a normal, independent state? Very little, indeed. Of course there is material enough. There rarely was a time when so much ink was wasted on decrees and bills and pamphlets discussing the decrees. Everything of any importance was referred to the voters, and therefore had to be printed. But of what value is all this material? Some day it may be used for a learned doctor's thesis. To the general historical reader it is without any interest. In name the republic was still a free commonwealth. In practice — we have repeatedly stated this before—it was a French province. The First Consul ruled her and gave his orders either through the Batavian minister in Paris or the French minister in The Hague. That such orders were ever disobeyed we do not find recorded. At times there was a little grumbling, but even if the noise thereof ever penetrated to Paris it was dismissed as the silly complaint of a lot of tradespeople who were always kicking. That was part of their business. The best answer to their remonstrances was an increase in the taxes—5 per cent. on this, 3 per cent. more on that, 20 per cent. on another article. Income, windows, light, air, newspapers, bread, tobacco, cheese—there was not an item that did not contribute toward making Napoleon's rule a success. For five years the republic, with its twelve executive gentlemen, ambled along. The better elements no longer appeared either in the assembly or in the colleges of the voters. The government gradually was left entirely to professional politicians of the lowest sort. The legislative body at once reflected this attitude of the more intelligent people to abstain from participation in the political life of their country.

It is true that the peace of Amiens made a momentary end to the French wars and brought about peace between England and the republic. But before the Dutch ships had been able to reach the Indian island war had again broken out, the colonies were once more captured by the British, and the Dutch coast was again blockaded. Bound to France by its disastrous treaty of 1796, the republic must follow the fate of the great sister republic. The people (we are now in 1803) had since the beginning of the revolution produced 600,000,000 guilders in taxes. They tried to convince the First Consul that they could not go on doing this forever. He, however, was able to suggest quite a wonderful remedy for their difficulties. The Batavian Republic must strengthen her fleet until she could defeat England and take back the colonies which that perfidious country had stolen. Very well! But the fleet could not be improved without further millions, and so the republic moved in a vicious circle which led to nowhere in particular but cost money all along that eternal line.

For a change, and to remind them of their duty, the Consul sent urgent demands for honorary dotations, for extraordinary dotations, for special dotations, or whatever names he chose to give to those official thefts.

The Exchange upon such occasions would fly into a panic. Couriers would race madly along the roads between The Hague and Paris. But invariably the end of all this commotion was a new command for the republic to pay up and be very quick about it, too. Continually during those five years do we hear Napoleon's warning: "If the republic refuses to pay, and refuses to obey my orders in general, I shall turn it into a French department."

Schimmelpenninck, very moderate in his views, not too enthusiastic about the Batavian form of government, and rather in favour of the American system, during those very difficult days represented his country in Paris as its diplomatic agent. He had to carry the brunt of those wordy battles about the increased taxes. Napoleon may not have been able to speak French grammatically; but he certainly did have at his command a varied and choice collection of Parisian and Corsican Billingsgate. Continually in his correspondence with the Batavian Republic the Consul flew into a rage, called everybody very unpolite names, insulted the persons and the families of the members of the executive, told everybody indiscriminately what he thought of them or what he would do to their worthless persons. The browbeaten executives could do nothing but bow very low, accept the insults in an humble spirit, and express their invariable loyalty to the man who called them a bunch of sneaking grafters devoid of honour, energy, and patriotism.

This policy after a while had a very bad influence upon the Batavian Government. People lost all hope for the future. All desire to start upon new enterprises was killed. What was the use? The fruits of one's industry were taken away for the benefit of the French armies. And any day might be the last. The Consul might have had a bad night, he might be out of temper, and "finis" then for the Republic of the Free Batavians.

The year 1805 came, and with it a demand for 15,000,000 guilders to be given as a loan, returnable in four years. Fortunately it was before the battle of Jena had shown the weakness of Prussia, and Napoleon did not dare to attack the republic too openly. But he had made up his mind that the present weak form of government could not continue. The large executive must be abolished, and a single man, be he a French general or a member of the House of Bonaparte, must be made the head of the republic. The republic alone seemed unable to walk. Napoleon would give her somebody for her support. Unfortunately there was no general available, and all the consular brethren were engaged elsewhere. For lack of a Frenchman a Hollander must take the job. There was only one Hollander whom the Consul (the Emperor since a few months) could trust and for whom he had some personal liking. That was the Batavian minister, Schimmelpenninck. The latter, however, had no ambitions of this sort and refused the offer to become Proconsul of the Republic. He pleaded ill health, a weakening eyesight. Napoleon refused to listen to his excuses. If Schimmelpenninck were unwilling to accept, then France must annex the republic. Whereupon the Batavian minister, inspired by the unselfish interest which he took in his fatherland, agreed to accept the difficult position. He sadly drove to The Hague along the heavy roads of a very severe winter, and he informed the twelve citizens of the executive body what the Emperor intended to do with him and with them and with the Batavian Republic. The executive must resign at once. As an executive body it had proved itself to be too large and too ineffective. As a legislative body it had done nothing of any importance. It must go. A new constitution (a fourth one, if you please), more centralized and more after the French pattern, must be adopted.

The executive, mild as lambs, approved of everything, said yea and amen to all the proposals of the Emperor. It informed the legislative body of the contemplated changes and advised the legislators that the appointment of Schimmelpenninck as Proconsul was the only way out of the difficulty. The legislative body, just to keep up appearances, deliberated for six whole days. Then it expressed its full approval of everything the Emperor proposed to do with them and for them. The new constitution, made in Paris, was forwarded to The Hague by parcels post, was put into type, and was brought before the electorate. The voters by this time did not care what happened or who governed them so long as they themselves were only left in peace. And when the time came for them to express their opinion 139 men out of a total of 350,000, took the trouble to say no, while less than one-twenty-fifth of the voting part of the population took the trouble of expressing an affirmative opinion. Out of every hundred voters, ninety-six stayed quietly at home. It saved trouble.

Schimmelpenninck

XX.

SCHIMMELPENNINCK

Schimmelpenninck made himself no false ideals about his high office, which placed him, a simple man, in the palace of the Noordeinde (the present royal palace of the kings of the Netherlands), which surrounded him with a lifeguard of 1,500 men, gave him the title of Raadpensionaris, encompassed him with an iron circle of regal etiquette, and provided him with many things which were quite as much against the essential character of the Hollanders as against his own personal tastes.

For himself, the new Raadpensionaris asked for very little. He was careful not to appoint a single one of his relatives to any public office, and tried in the most impartial way to gather all the more able elements of every party around himself. He appointed his cabinet and selected his advisers from the unionists and the federalists, but most of all from among the moderates.

The Raadpensionaris in this new commonwealth of Napoleon's making was a complete autocrat. Provisions had been made for a legislative body of nineteen men, to be appointed by the different provinces; but this legislature, which was to meet twice a year and had resumed the old title of their High and Mightinesses, the Estates General, amounted to nothing at all. At the very best it was an official gallery which applauded the acts of the Raadpensionaris.

This dignitary and his ministers worked meanwhile with the greatest energy. A most capable man was appointed to be secretary of the treasury. He actually managed to reduce the deficit by several millions, and began to take steps to put the country upon a sound financial basis. Napoleon, however, did not fancy the idea of the republic getting out of debt too completely. If anything were to be done in this line he proposed an immediate reduction of the public debt. In the end, so he reasoned, such a reduction would be a benefit. At the present moment, as far as the Emperor could make out, the people through their taxes paid the money which at the end of the year came back to them through their investments in public funds. Reduce the national debt and you will reduce taxation. But however much his Majesty might advocate his pet plans, the commercial soul of the republic refused to listen to these proposals of such dangerous financial sleight-of-hand and the people rather suffered a high taxation than submit to an open confession of inability to manage their own treasury.

The army, for which the Raadpensionaris personally had very little love, was developed into a small but very efficient corps. This had to be done. Unless the army were well looked after, Napoleon threatened to introduce conscription in the republic, and to avert this national calamity people were willing to make further sacrifices and support an army consisting of volunteers. The navy, too, was put into good shape. A new man was at work in this department, a certain Verhuell, an ardent revolutionist, and the Hollander who seems to have had the greatest influence over the Emperor. During all the events between 1800 and 1812 Verhuell acted as the unofficial intermediary between the republic and the Emperor. He was a good sailor. In a number of engagements with the British his ships ably held their own water. But the Dutch fleet alone was far too small to tackle England, and the French fleet was soon lost sight of through the battle of Trafalgar.

Came the year 1806 and the defeat of the coalition. Ulm and Austerlitz were not only disasters to the Austrians; they had their effect upon the republic. Napoleon, complete master of the European continent, parcelled out its territory in new states and created new kingdoms and duchies without any regard to the personal wishes of the subjects of these artificial nations.

The Batavian Republic had been spared through the sentimentality of the French revolutionists. For several years it had been left alone because Napoleon still had to respect the wishes of Prussia and Austria. Now Prussia and Austria had been reduced to third-class powers, and the Emperor could treat the republic as he wished to. He sent for his Dutch man Friday, Verhuell, and talked about his plans. "Had the admiral noticed that during the war with the European coalition the French armies in the republic had been under command of his Majesty's brother, the Prince Louis Napoleon?" Mr. Verhuell had noticed the presence of the young member of the House of Bonaparte. So had everybody else. "Did Mr. Verhuell know what this presence meant?" Mr. Verhuell could guess. So could everybody else. Very well! Mr. Verhuell could go to The Hague and inform his fellow-citizens that they might choose between asking for the Prince Louis Bonaparte as their king or becoming a French department. With this cheerful message Mr. Verhuell repaired to The Hague, just a year after the Raadpensionaris had travelled that same road to assume the consulship of the republic. The Batavians were obliged to accept their fate with Christian resignation. Opposition of ten thousand Dutch recruits against half a million well-trained French soldiers was impossible. Furthermore, it is a doubtful question whether the people would have fought for their independence. There had been too many years full of disaster. The spirit of the people had been broken. They were now willing to accept anything. The only question to decide was how to get through this new comedy with some semblance of the old dignity. Schimmelpenninck, who was a very constitutional person, called together the grand council, consisting of the legislative body, the council of state, and a number of high dignitaries, and proposed that the new plan be submitted to the voters. The grand council voted him down directly. As it was, there had been too many elections already. The people must be left out of this affair. No good would come from their interference, anyway.

Schimmelpenninck arrives at The Hague

And forthwith the council resorted to the old Dutch expedient of procrastination. It sent a delegation to Paris to see the Emperor. Meanwhile, something might turn up. It did turn up—in the form of an ultimatum from his Majesty. He refused to receive the delegation, but sent word by Verhuell that the republic was given just eight days in which to repair to Paris and ask the Emperor for the favour of his brother as their king. If they were a day late the country would be turned into a French department.

On the 3rd of May, 1806, the grand council in The Hague agreed to all the French demands. The ex-bishop of Autun, the Rev. Mr. Talleyrand, had been appointed by Napoleon to draw up a constitution for the new kingdom. That was easy enough. After two weeks he could send the finished article to the grand council for its approval. The council approved; but Schimmelpenninck denounced the whole proceeding as being unconstitutional, and refused to sign the document. The council signed it over his head, and returned the paper to Paris. Then Schimmelpenninck protested to the French minister, and told him that he could not possibly justify the actions of the council. The minister said that he was sorry, but that nothing could be done about it, since the document was back in Paris. Whereupon Schimmelpenninck resigned and retired to his country place, declining all further participation in his country's political affairs. He lived until the year 1825, long enough to see his beloved land regain its independence and finally benefit by many of the reforms which he himself had helped to bring about.

The Speaker of the legislative body was selected to succeed the Raadpensionaris. Together with his colleagues of the grand council he now had the dishonour of arranging the last details of the farce which had been ordered by Paris.

On the 5th of June, of the year 1806, the Emperor Napoleon graciously deigned to receive a deputation from among the Batavian people who had come to Paris to ask his Majesty to present them with a king. The reason for this request, according to the delegates themselves, was the weakness of their country, which did not allow them to defend themselves against their enemies.

His Majesty, from a high tower of condescension, agreed to

honour the petitioners with a favourable reply. His Majesty's own brother would be appointed king of the Batavians.

The new king, an amiable man, but not in the least desirous to be made king of Holland (having such difficulties in governing his own wife that he could not well bother about the additional duties of an entire kingdom), was then asked to step forward. He humbly listened to his brother's admonition never to "cease being a Frenchman," and answered that he would accept the crown and do his best, "since his Majesty had been pleased to order it so." That was all. The Batavian delegation was dismissed. The new king retired, to go to his unhappy home; but before he left the hall M. Talleyrand called him back and handed him a copy of the constitution of his new kingdom. Would his Majesty kindly peruse the document at his own leisure and make such suggestions as might occur to him? His Majesty took the document. He was sure that it was all right. His brother had approved of it. A few days later Louis packed his wife and his children in the royal coach and slowly rolled to his new domains. The people in the cities through which he passed gazed at this ready-made monarch with a dull curiosity. They wondered what this experiment would bring them.

Louis Napoleon

XXI.

KING LOUIS OF HOLLAND

The new king was twenty-eight years old, not especially good looking, kind-hearted, not specially clever, a little vain (as who would not be who was made a king overnight), filled with the best of intentions toward his new subjects, and none too fond of his brother. The difference between the two Bonapartes was great. Louis was a gentleman, Napoleon tried to be.

The wife of the new king, whose morals were diametrically opposed to her looks (she was very handsome), was a stepdaughter of the Emperor. She hated her new country and its unelegant inhabitants. She was thoroughly indifferent about her husband's fortunes, and she spent most of her time in Paris and far away from her husband's court.

The new king made a tour of inspection of his possessions, and then settled down to rule. First of all, he tried to learn a little Dutch and to understand something of the history of his adopted country. These attempts were not brilliantly successful, but the patient people heard of them and were happy. "At last," so they said, "we have a nice, good man to be our king, and his brother will leave us alone."

The regents, meanwhile, who had been invisible as long as they were governed by one of their own people, now began to appear out of their hiding-places. They accepted this new imported Majesty with much better grace than they had received plain Mr. Schimmelpenninck. The son of an obscure lawyer and notary public in a little semi-barbarous island, of royal blood by the grace of his brother, could command the respect which had been refused the member of an old and honourable Dutch family. The palace of his Majesty King Louis became the centre to which flocked all those who desired to become groom of the bedchamber or assistant master of the horse. Louis was not averse to gold lace, and encouraged these high aspirations, created nobles, gave orders, and filled his brother's heart with amusement, mixed with contemptible scorn, by the creation of Dutch marshals. A few among the old families, notably our former friend Van Hogendorp, preferred obscurity to the reflected splendour of a Bonapartistic throne. But they were the exceptions, not the rule.

The new constitution which King Louis had brought along with him somewhere in his luggage was unpacked and was put into practice. It proved to be a concise little document, written with Napoleonic brevity. It contained only seventy-nine articles. All power was invested in the king, who was assisted by a cabinet consisting of a council of state and a number of ministers. The legislative chamber of thirty-eight members was to convene once a year for two months, and, like its predecessors, it could only veto or accept bills. It could not propose or amend the laws.

Schimmelpenninck was offered the speakership of the assembly for life, but he refused. Van Hogendorp was offered a seat in the council of state, but he declined. The members of the council and the ministers were then elected from among the able men belonging to the different parties. They were called upon to forget all former partisanship and to unite in one common cause, the resurrection of the poverty-stricken fatherland.

Theoretically, King Louis was much in favour of rigid economy. In practice, however, he proved to be a very costly monarch. It is true that he gave the people their money's worth. There were parades and elaborate coaches and gorgeous uniforms and fine outriders and all the other paraphernalia so dear to the heart of the gaping multitude. But soon the restlessness of a man who is miserably unhappy at home, and who will give anything for diversion, took hold of the poor king. He began to dislike his palace in The Hague, and moved to the house in the woods. Then he moved to Haarlem. Then he discovered that Haarlem was not central enough, and he moved to Utrecht. But Utrecht was too small and too dull, and he tried Amsterdam. Now all this moving on a regal scale cost enormous sums of money. Besides that, the king wished to furnish his palaces with costly furniture, hang splendid tapestries upon the walls, surround himself with fine works of art.

But these thousands were insignificant compared to the millions which were being spent upon the army and the navy. Verhuell, the man after Napoleon's heart, had received orders to make the navy into a good one. He had obeyed his orders promptly, but it had cost a pretty penny. And the army, now that Napoleon was fighting everybody on the European continent, had to be kept up to an ever-increasing standard of efficiency. The revenues, on the other hand, fell below the disheartening average of former years. For Holland, as a dependency of France, had to obey the absurd rules against English goods with which Napoleon hoped to starve Great Britain into submission.

Together with King Louis there had appeared in the republic a veritable army of French spies. They were under orders to prevent smuggling, and to see that the laws against British goods be strictly enforced. Rotterdam and several cities which had prolonged their economic existence through wholesale smuggling were now ruined. Every year it became more difficult to raise the extraordinary taxes for the army and navy. The secretary of the treasury at his first audience with King Louis had been able to inform the monarch that the state of the country's finances was as follows: In cash, 205,000 guilders. Deficit on this year's debt, 35,000,000. The secretary of the treasury thereafter became a nightmare to the poor king. Every month he appeared with a more doleful story. Every so many weeks he approached the king with new and involved plans to bring about some improvements in the finances of the kingdom. Louis, who shared his brother's dislike for economics, was terribly bored. At last, in self-defence, he dismissed his minister of finances, the very capable Gogel, who had begun life as a clerk in a bookstore and had worked his way up through sheer ability. The new secretary of the treasury was less of a persistent bore, but the economic condition of the country grew worse instead of better.

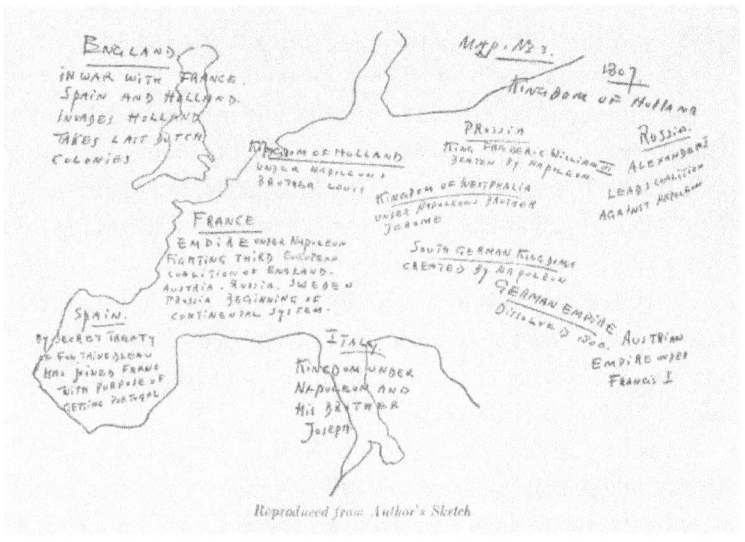

1807. Kingdom of Holland.

What more can we say of the rule of this well-meaning monarch? He was the receiver appointed in a bankrupt business. It was a wonder that he could maintain himself for four whole years. He was not a man who made friends easily. A rapidly developing sense of his own dignity gradually isolated him from those men who meant well with the king and the country. He tried to improve the arts and sciences by founding an academy. But painters and poets cannot be made to order, and his academy did not flourish.

Agriculture and commerce were encouraged by the construction of a number of excellent roads and the making of several important polders. But with all foreign markets, except the French, closed to them, the products of the farmer and the manufacturer could not be exported. The good intentions were all there, but the adverse circumstances were too powerful. The king was tender-hearted. When there was a national calamity, a fire, or an inundation, the king might be seen on the nearest dike trying to fish people out of the flood. But with Christian charity alone a nation cannot be made prosperous.

The king tried to get rid of the French influence. His wife, who intrigued against him with her cousin, the French minister, opposed his independent plans. The king then tried to get rid of his wife; but brother Napoleon, who contemplated divorcing his own wife, in order to marry into a better family, did not like the idea of two separations in the family at the same time, and Louis was obliged to stay married. He then tried to get rid of the French minister, but Napoleon supported his envoy and refused to recall so devoted and useful a servant.

It was England which finally spoiled King Louis' last chances. After a long preparation, during which Napoleon had frequently taken occasion to warn his brother, the English fleet crossed the North Sea and attacked the Dutch island of Walcheren preparatory to an assault upon Antwerp, Napoleon's great naval base. The strong town of Flushing, after a bombardment which incidentally destroyed every house in that city, was taken by the British forces, and the advance against Antwerp was begun. The French, however, had been able to make full preparations for defence. Bernadotte had inundated the country surrounding the Belgian fortress, and the British were obliged to stay where they were, on the Zeeland Islands. As usual, Holland paid the expenses. When finally the malarial fever had driven the English out of the country, the plundered provinces had to be kept alive by public charity.

Napoleon was furious. His pet scheme, the glorious harbour of Antwerp, had almost fallen into English hands. Why had not his brother taken measures to prevent such a thing? "Holland was merely a British dependency where the English deposited of their wares in perfect safety. The Emperor's own brother was an ally of England. Why does he not equip an army strong enough to resist such British aggressions? The Kingdom of Holland says that it is too poor to pay more for an army. Lies, all lies. Holland is rich. It is the richest nation on the continent. But every time the pockets of their High and Mightinesses are touched they make a terrible noise and plead poverty. Don't listen to their complaints. Make them pay! Do you hear? Make them pay!" And so on, and so on. There exists an entire correspondence to this effect. Louis answered as best he could. The Emperor was not satisfied. He sent for his brother to come to Paris. Louis went. When he arrived, Napoleon scolded him openly before his entire court, before the new wife which his armies had obtained for him in Vienna. The humiliation was great, but still Louis refused to resign and deliver the country of which he had grown fond to the tender mercies of his august brother. Even when, in March of the year 1810, Napoleon, by a sudden decree, annexed part of the south of the kingdom, Louis refused to give in and depart. For a while he contemplated armed resistance to the French armies. Krayenhoff worked on a plan for the inundation of Amsterdam. A number of generals who were suspected of French sentiments were dismissed. The idea, however, was given up as altogether too impossible. The Dutch ministers would not follow their king. The council of state refused to give him money for such purposes. And Napoleon gathered a large army and began to move his troops in the direction of Amsterdam.

Louis, despairing of everything for the future of himself and his country, would not continue to rule under such circumstances. On the 1st of July, 1810, he abdicated in favour of his small son. The child, just seven years old, was to be king under the guardianship of his mother, the admiral, Verhuell, and a number of the leading members of the cabinet.

On the night of the 2nd of June Louis, under the incognito of a Count of Leu, left his palace in Haarlem and departed forever from his kingdom. In the year 1846 he died in Livorno. Six years later his son ascended the French throne as Napoleon III.

News of the abdication reached Paris at the very moment that the troops of Napoleon took possession of Amsterdam. One week later, on the 9th of July, Napoleon signed the decree of annexation. The little bit of mud deposited upon the shores of the North Sea by the French rivers, and for some years known as the Dutch Republic, ceased to be an independent state and became a minor French province.

Napoleon visits Amsterdam

XXII.

THE DEPARTMENT FORMERLY CALLED HOLLAND

For the next three years the Hollanders went to the French school. The teachers were severe masters, but the pupils learned a lot. The Batavian Republic, and even the kingdom of Louis Napoleon, had been but continuations of the old partisan struggles of the former republics. The new state of affairs wiped the slate clean. The government came into the hands of French superiors who trained the lower Dutch officials in the new methods of governmental administration, who insisted upon running the state as they would a business firm, and to whom the petty considerations of former partisanship meant absolutely nothing. Uniform laws for the entire country, which the different assemblies had not been able to institute, were drawn up and were enforced upon all Hollanders with equal severity. The old system of jurisprudence, different for every little province, town, or village, was replaced by one single system. The Code Napoleon became the law for all.

The old trouble with the armed forces which had put the republic under the obligation of hiring mercenaries was now done away with. The new conscription took in all able-bodied citizens, put them all in the same uniform, and gave them all the same chance to serve their country and be killed for its glory.

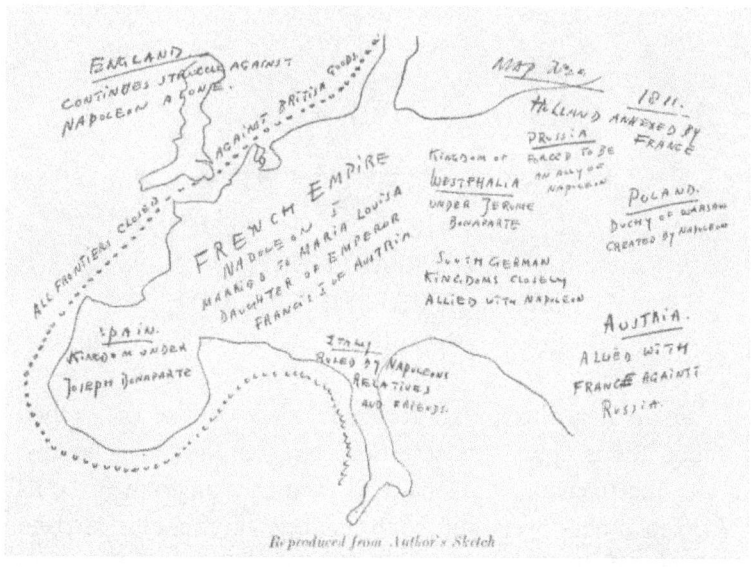

1811. Holland annexed by France.

But, best of all, that old atmosphere in which a man from one village had looked upon his nearest neighbour from another village as his worst enemy was at last cleared away. A man might have been an Orangeist or a federalist or a Jacobin, he might have believed in the supreme right of the state or the divine right of his own family—before the new ruler this made no difference. Napoleon asked no questions about the past. He insisted upon duties toward the future. Before that capital N all men became equal, because they all were inferiors. Promotion could be won only by ability and through faithful service. Family influence no longer counted.

Humble names were suddenly elevated if their possessors showed themselves worthy of the Emperor's confidence.

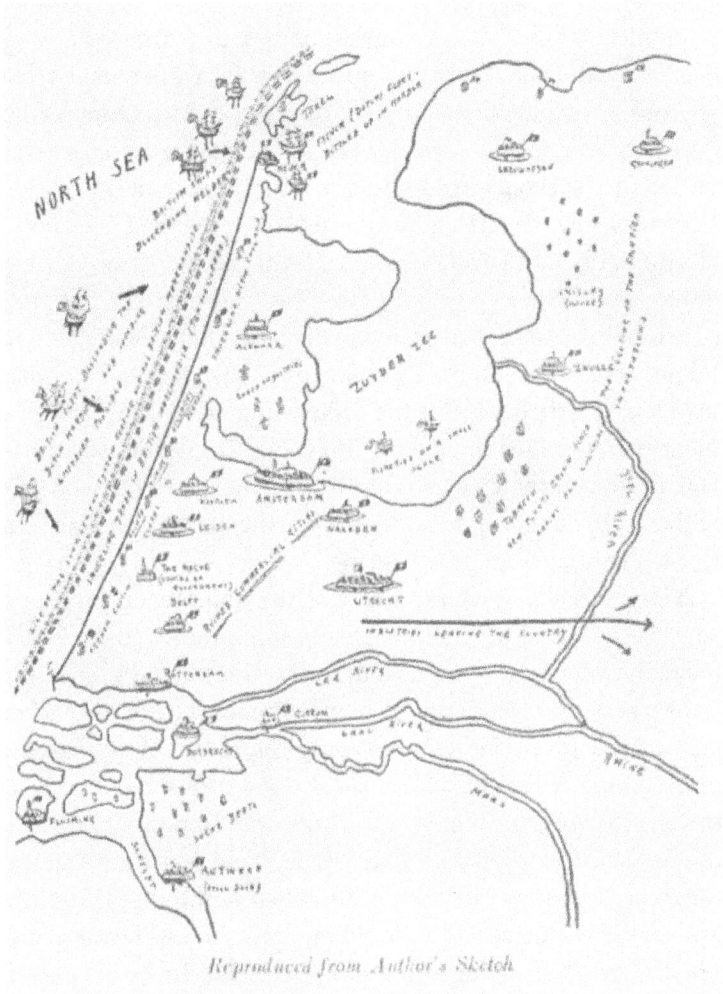

Reproduced from Author's Sketch.

The whole country was thrown into one gigantic melting-pot of foreign make and stirred by a foreign master without any respect for the separate ingredients out of which he was trying to brew his one and indivisible French Empire.

The new French province was arbitrarily divided into

departments. The old provincial names and frontiers were discontinued. Each little department was called after some river or brook which happened to flow through it. At its head came a prefect, invariably a Frenchman. A French governor-general resided in The Hague to exercise the supreme command.

Fortunately the first governor-general, the French General Lebrun, Duke of Plaisance, was a decent old man who did his best to make the sudden change from Hollander into Frenchman as little painful to the subject as possible. And his subjects, if they did not actually love the old gentleman, always treated him with respect and deference. But the same thing cannot be said of a majority of the French prefects. They were insolent adventurers who had fought their way up from among the ranks, but who had neither understanding nor affection for the despised Hollanders over whom they were called to rule.

A large French army came to Holland and French garrisons were placed in all of the more important cities. Churches and hospitals were hastily turned into barracks, and the soldiers made themselves entirely at home. French customs officers were placed in all the villages along the coast. They watched all harbours. A French soldier sailed on every fishing smack to prevent smuggling. The entire village was responsible for his safe return. French police spies made their entry into Dutch society and kept a control over all Dutch families. The French language was officially introduced into all schools, theatres, and newspapers. The universities, except the one in Leiden, were abolished or changed into secondary schools. What gradually made the French rule so unpopular, and what finally made it so universally hated, was not the introduction of an entirely new form of government. The political innovations were hailed by the thinking part of the nation with considerable joy. Foreign influence brought about improvements which the people themselves, with their age-old political prejudices, could not have instituted. It was not the ever-increasing severity of the taxes nor the unpleasant presence of a large French army which made the people regard Napoleon as the incarnation of Antichrist. The opposition to everything French began the moment Napoleon started to interfere with those undefinable parts of daily life which we call the national character, or, still shorter, the "nationality." Napoleon, himself an Italian ruling over Frenchmen, does not seem to have understood this sentiment at all. Under different circumstances he would just as happily have made his career in Russia or in China. His failures in every country date from the moment when he attacked the nationality of his enemies. The Dutch or the Spanish or the German child could be made to speak French in school, but the soldiers of the Emperor could not force the mother of the child to teach it French when first it began to prattle. The Dutch citizen could be forced to read a newspaper printed in French and to attend a church where the sermon was preached in French, but he could not be made to think in that language. Dutch nationality, driven violently from the public places, hid itself in the home, and there entrenched itself behind impregnable barriers. At home the nation suffered, and in the proscribed language talked of the future and the better times which must certainly follow. For when the year 1812 came the nation had reached a depth of misery so very low that things simply could not be worse. The most despondent pessimist by the very hopeless condition of affairs was turned into an optimist. Trade and commerce were gone; smuggling was impossible; factories stood empty and deserted; no dividends were paid. By imperial decree the national debt had been reduced to one third of its actual size. Families whose income had been three thousand guilders now received one thousand. Those who had had one thousand became paupers. One fourth of the people of Amsterdam were kept alive by public charities, until finally the charities themselves had no more to give, and had to go into bankruptcy. Another fourth of the population, while not absolutely dependent, received partial support. The other half of the people were obliged to give up everything that was not absolutely necessary for just simple existence. They dismissed their servants, they sold their horses, they refrained from buying books and articles of luxury.

Departure of Gardes d'Honneur from Amsterdam

Then came the sudden blow of the conscription. First of all, the young men of twenty-one years of age were taken into the army. Then the conscription was extended upward and downward. Finally, those who had celebrated their nineteenth birthday in the year 1788 were forced to take up arms. The few boys who drew a high lot and were free if they belonged to the higher classes were honoured with a patent of a sub-altern in his Majesty's personal bodyguard. If they were poor they were used for some extra duty, as hospital soldiers, or were enlisted under some flimsy pretext. In short, there was no way of escape. After a while there was not a family in the land, be it rich or poor, whose sons or brothers were not serving the Emperor in his armies, and in far-away countries were risking their lives for a cause as vile as any that has ever been fought for.

Came the year 1812 and the preparations for the expedition against Russia. Fifteen thousand Dutch troops were divided among the French armies as hussars, infantry, artillery, or engineers. They were not allowed to form one Dutch contingent for fear of possible mutiny. As a minor part of the enormous army of invasion they marched across the Russian plains. A few of the men managed to desert and to join the English troops or the irregular bands which were beginning to operate in Germany. The others were frozen to death or were killed in battle. The Fourth Dutch Hussars charged a Russian battery and was reduced to forty-six men. This was at the beginning of September. A month later the Third Grenadiers was decimated until only forty men were left. Of the four regiments of infantry of the line only one came back as such. The others, shot to pieces, reduced by cold and starvation, gradually wandered home as part of that endless stream of starving men who early in 1813 began to beg for bread along the roads of eastern Prussia. Of the Second Lancers only two men ever saw their fatherland again. The Thirty-third Light Infantry was practically annihilated, until only twenty-five men survived, and they as prisoners in Russia. Of two hundred Hollanders serving in the One Hundred and Twenty-fourth Infantry not a single one ever returned.

It was a terrible story, but it did not affect the Emperor. His answer to the catastrophe was a demand for more troops. The sailors were taken from the fleet. Young boys and old men were mustered into the army. Here and there Dutch farmers, first robbed of their money, then of their possessions, finally deprived of their sons, resisted, took pitchforks and killed a few gendarmes. Immediate reprisals followed. The culprits were stood against the nearest trees and shot, the sons were marched off to the army, and the farms were confiscated.

One hundred years ago, at the moment we are writing this chapter, on the 18th of November, 1813, old man Bluecher, cursing and swearing at the Corsican blackguard, whirled his cavalry against the left flank of the French army, smashed it to pieces, and changed Napoleon's victory of Leipzig into a defeat. After a week the first news of the Emperor's defeat reached the republic. Officially it was not announced until some months later. Even then it made little impression. The people were too dejected to rejoice. They had heard of such defeats before, and invariably the announcement had been followed by a masterstroke on the part of the terrible Emperor and a rehabilitation of his military prestige. Here and there in the universities and in the schools some teachers began to whisper that the days of slavery might be soon over. But nobody dared to listen. Only a fool or a college professor could believe in the final victory of the allies.

It was now near the middle of November. Most of the French troops had been called to the frontiers. A few regiments of custom-house men had been left behind, and a few companies of either very old or very young men. It was a dangerous moment. In the east the allies were rapidly approaching the Dutch frontiers. The possession of the Dutch harbours would mean direct communication with England and an open road to the British goods and the British money of which the allies were in such desperate need. That Holland on this occasion was not conquered by the allies as French territory was entirely due to the energy of one man, bravely supported by a small number of able friends.

Gysbert Karel Van Hogendorp

XXIII.

LIBERATION

The name of Van Hogendorp has been frequently mentioned before. First of all as the adviser of the Princess Wilhelmina during her attempt to cause some spontaneous enthusiasm for her husband, who had been driven out of his province of Holland by the Patriots. After the year 1795 we have been able to call attention repeatedly to the conduct of this excellent gentleman, who was most obstinate in his fidelity to his given word and refused to consider himself freed from the oath of allegiance which he once had sworn to the Stadholder. He simply refused all overtures from the side of the revolution, and later from King Louis, and lived a forgotten existence in a big and dignified house. He had a brother, Charles, who thought him to be altogether too idealistic, and who had accepted a position under the Emperor and was at this time a well-known general. For the rest, and outside of his own family, Van Hogendorp for many years did not associate intimately with a great number of people. The last years had been very dangerous to those who engaged conspicuously in social life. French spies might have wondered why Mr. So and So was so very fond of the company of his neighbour, and some fine night both gentlemen might have been lifted out of their beds, their correspondence confiscated, and for weeks or even months they might have been kept in jail. It was one of the measures of the Emperor himself which directly drove a number of prominent Dutch families into a closer union. The creation of the so-called Guards of Honour meant that all the boys of the higher classes, who formerly had been often allowed to send substitutes, now had to enter the army personally. There had been very great opposition. The police had had to interfere and had been obliged to drag many of the recruits to the barracks. Arrests had been made and fines had been imposed, and out of sheer misery many families who had not been intimate before now came to know each other more closely. It was among those unfortunate people that Van Hogendorp first seems to have looked for associates and confederates in his plans for a revolution against the French Government. Of course, of a revolution which even in the smallest degree shall resemble the rebellion against Spain, we shall see nothing. Everything in Holland during those years was on a small scale. The nation was old and weakened and tottered around with difficulty. Not for a moment must we imagine a situation where enthusiastic Patriots rush to the standard of rebellion. All in all we shall see perhaps a dozen men who are willing to take the slightest personal risk and who by sheer force of their character shall compel the rest of the nation to follow their example. It was a revolution in spite of the Dutch people, not through them.

It is not merely for convenience sake that we take Van Hogendorp as the centre. He was really the man of imagination who, long before the French had been beaten, understood that this Napoleonic empire, built upon violence and deceit, could not survive—must inevitably perish, and that soon the time would come for his own country to regain its independence. He had studied the situation with such care that he was able to time his uprising very precisely. When the news came of the battle of Leipzig, Van Hogendorp was engaged upon a rough draft of a new constitution for the benefit of the independent republic which he felt must soon materialize.

Now the expected had happened. Napoleon had been beaten and was in full flight. The allies were marching upon the French and Dutch frontiers. The next weeks would decide everything. It was a period of the greatest confusion. The Emperor, engaged in creating new armies out of almost impossible material, had no time to give orders to his outposts. The French army in the department formerly called Holland must help itself. The result of this ignorance about the general affairs in France and Germany was a hopeless diversity in false rumours. Every single hour, almost, the prefects in the provinces and the governor-general in The Hague were surprised by some new and terrible story. One moment a report was spread throughout the town that the Emperor was dead. The next day it was contradicted: the Emperor had merely gone crazy. The next day he was in his right mind again, but had been taken prisoner by the Cossacks, and the French had crossed the Rhine. After a while, however, some definite orders came from Paris. The French army must concentrate and try to defend the frontiers of France. Here was news indeed. On the evening of the 14th of November, 1813, the French troops in Amsterdam were packed in a number of boats and rowed away in a southern direction. Amsterdam was without a garrison. Immediately there followed a terrific explosion. The poor people, after so many years of misery and hunger, after so many months in which they had tasted neither coffee nor sugar, not to speak of tobacco, burst forth to take their revenge. The French soldiers were gone. The only visible sign of the hated foreign domination was the little wooden houses which up to that day had been occupied by the French douaniers. Half an hour after the last Frenchman had disappeared the air was red with the flames of those buildings, and the infuriated populace was dancing a wild gallop of joy around the cheerful bonfire.

But right here we come to one of the saddest parts of the year 1813. These insurgents, rebels, hoodlums, or whatever you wish to call them, received no support from above. The old spirit of the regents was still too strong. The higher classes saw this wild carousal, but instead of guiding it into an organized movement to be used against the French, they were terribly scared, thinking only of danger to their own property, and decided to stop the violent outbreak before further harm could be done. With promises of the splendid things that might happen to-morrow they got the people back into their slums. Then they quickly organized a volunteer police corps and made ready to keep the people in their proper place, and actually prevent further outbreaks. That the time had come to throw off the French yoke does not seem to have been apparent to the majority of the former regents, who hastened back to the town hall the moment the French burgomasters had left. They were scared, and they refused to budge. The French flag was kept flying on the public buildings. Napoleon might come back, and the regents were not going to be caught standing on a patriotic barricade waving Orange banners. The fame for the first open outbreak goes to the poor people of Amsterdam. But the old conservative classes of the city prevented the town from actually becoming the leader of this great movement for Holland's independence. Late in the evening of the 16th of November the news of the burning of the French custom-houses in Amsterdam reached The Hague. A few hours before the French governor had left the residence and had gone to Utrecht to be nearer the centre of the country. But several French troops and policemen had been left behind to keep order. At three o'clock of the night of the 17th, while the town was asleep, Van Hogendorp sent a messenger to the Dutch commander of the civic militia. The commander came, but regretted to report that his militia had been left entirely without arms by the French authorities, who suspected them of treason. The mayor was then appealed to. He was told of the danger that might occur should the common people attack the French troops. The militia must have arms to keep order. The mayor, who was a Hollander, readily gave the required permission. Just before sunrise the town guards were assembled in front of the old palace of the Stadholders. They were given arms and were told to keep themselves in readiness. That was the moment for which Van Hogendorp had waited.

With a large orange-coloured bow upon his hat, General Leopold van Limburg Stirum, the friend and chief fellow-conspirator of Van Hogendorp, suddenly appeared upon the public street. Slowly, with a crowd of admiring citizens behind him, he walked to the place where the militia waited. There he read a proclamation which Van Hogendorp had prepared beforehand:

"Holland is free. Long live the House of Orange. The French rule has come to an end. The sea is open, commerce revives, the past is forgotten. All old partisanship has ceased to be, and everything has been forgiven."

Proclamation of the new Government

Then the proclamation went on to indicate the new form of government. There would be founded a state in which all men of some importance would be able to take part, under the high leadership of the Prince of Orange. The militia listened with approval, then with beating drums and waving the Orange colours, which had not been seen for almost a generation, the soldiers marched through the excited town directly to the city hall. The old flag of the republic was hoisted on the tower of the church nearby. Within an hour the news of this wonderful event had spread throughout the town. On all sides, from doors and windows and upon roofs, the old red, white, and blue colours mixed with orange appeared. Orange ribbons, still disseminating a smell of the moth-chest in which they had lain hidden for so many years, appeared upon hats and around sleeves, were waved on canes, and put around the collars of the domestic canines. Spontaneous parades of orange-covered citizens began to wander through the streets.

The House of Van Hogendorp became the centre of all activity. In the afternoon of the same day Van Hogendorp and a number of his friends assumed the Provisional government, to handle the affairs of the state until the Prince of Orange should come to assume the highest leadership.

So far, the conspirators had been successful. The French soldiers showed no desire to oppose this popular movement, but they were still present in their barracks and constituted an element of grave danger. But in the afternoon the fisherfolk of Scheveningen, ultra-Orangeists, began to hear of the great doings in The Hague and enthusiastically made up their minds to join. And when the influx of this proverbially hard-fisted tribe became known to the French they decided that their number of five hundred was not sufficient to suppress the popular excitement. Hastily they packed their belongings and marched away in the direction of Utrecht. But before they had been gone half an hour, some two hundred Prussian grenadiers deserted and returned to The Hague, where they were received with open arms, and where they joined the populace with loud hoorays for the Prince of Orange and the hospitable Dutch nation.

Mere shouting, however, although a very necessary part of a revolution, has never yet brought about a victory. It was necessary to do some more substantial work than to cause a popular outbreak of enthusiasm. There must be order and a foundation upon which the new authorities should be able to construct a stable form of government. Van Hogendorp, therefore, took the next necessary step and hastily called upon all the former regents who could be reached to come and deliberate with him upon the establishment of a legitimate provisional form of government. Right there his difficulties began. The regents refused to come. They, like their brethren in Amsterdam, were afraid. Napoleon was invincible. They knew it. He was certain to regain the lost ground, and then he would come and take his revenge. And as far as they were concerned, the regents intended to stay at home. Only a few of them dared to come forward.

Amsterdam at this first meeting was represented by one man. His name was Falck. He was a *homo novus*, but by far the most capable of those who appeared at the house of Van Hogendorp, and he was at once selected to be the secretary of the meeting. Falck understood that such a poor beginning was worse than no revolution at all. The country must not return to the old bad conditions. The former regents had shown their lack of interest. A meeting must be called together of men from among all parties. Accordingly, on the 20th of November, a general meeting of notabilities from among all the former political parties was called together. It was not much more successful than the first one. The people distrusted it profoundly. They thought that there was to be a repetition of the old Estates General and that the conservative elements would again be in the majority. What was worse, the members of this informal convention had no confidence in themselves. Half a dozen were willing to go ahead. The others hesitated. They wanted to proceed slowly until they should know what would happen to the allies and what would become of Napoleon. The country had no army, it had no money, it had no credit.

In vain did Van Hogendorp talk to each member individually, in vain did he and his friends try every possible means of personal persuasion. The conservative elements were still too strong. The regents preached against more revolution. The French had been bad enough, but they did not wish to come once more under the domination of their own common people.

In this emergency all sorts of desperate remedies were resorted to. A British merchantman appeared before the coast near Scheveningen. At once Van Hogendorp sent word to the captain and asked him to put on his full uniform as a British militia officer and with a few of his men parade the streets of The Hague and Rotterdam. In this way the report would become current that a British auxiliary squadron had appeared before the coast. The captain did his best, and put on all his spangles. He did some good, but not so very much. Next, the leaders in The Hague asked for volunteers to form a Dutch army. Six hundred and thirty men answered the summons. Badly equipped and armed, they were marched to Amsterdam, where they were joined by a company of militia under the ever-active Falck. They arrived just in time. The next day the first advance guard of the army of the allies, a company of Cossacks, appeared before the gates of the town, and it was by the merest piece of luck that Amsterdam could welcome them as friends and need not open her gates to them as conquerors.

But withal, the situation was most precarious. In the north Verhuell held the fleet and threatened the Dutch coast. In the south all the principal cities were in French hands. In the centre of the country the French had fortified themselves considerably and even made frequent sallies upon the territory of the rebels, which cost the latter considerably in men and money. Finally, in the far east, Bluecher was preparing to invade the republic and make her territory the scene of his battles. For a moment it seemed that all the trouble had been for no purpose. Only one thing could save the situation. The Prince of Orange must come, must inspire the people with greater diligence for the good cause, and must take command of the disorganized forces.

Question: Where is the Prince? Nobody knew. He might be in England, but then, again, he might be with the allies somewhere along the Rhine. Messengers had been sent to London and to Frankfort. Those who went to Frankfort did not find the Prince, but they found the commanders of the allies and had the good sense to tell a fine yarn—how Holland had freed itself, and how the French had been ignominiously driven out. As a matter of fact, the Prince was in England, and in London, on the 21st of November, he heard how his arrival was eagerly awaited and how he must cross the North Sea at once. Five days later, well provided with men and money, he left the British coast on the frigate *Warrior*. An easterly wind, which nineteen years before had driven his father safely across the waters, delayed his voyage. For four whole days his ship tacked against this breeze. One British ship with 300 marines landed on the Dutch coast on the 27th, but nothing was heard of the Prince. The anxiety in Holland grew.

The fisher fleet of Scheveningen was sent out cruising in front of the coast to try to get in touch with the British fleet. But the days came and the days went by and no news was reported which might appease the general anxiety. Finally, on the morning of the 30th of November, the rumour spread suddenly through The Hague that the British fleet had been sighted. The Prince was coming! Then the people went forth to meet their old beloved Prince of Orange. Everything else was now forgotten. Along the same road where almost twenty years before they had gone to bid farewell to the father whom they had driven away, they now went to hail the son as their saviour.

At noon of Friday, the 30th, the *Warrior* came in sight. The same fisherman who eighteen years before had taken William to the ship which was to conduct him into his exile was now chosen to carry the new sovereign through the surf. With orange ribbons on his horses, with his coat covered with the same faithful colour, the old man drove through the waves. At four o'clock of the afternoon a sloop carrying the Prince left the British man-of-war. Half an hour later William landed.

The shore once more was black with people. The old road to The Hague was again lined with thousands of people. Little boys had climbed up into trees. Small children were lifted high by their mothers that they might get a glimpse of the hallowed person of a member of the House of Orange. A few people, from sheer excitement, shrieked their welcome. They were at once commanded to be silent. The moment was too solemn for such an expression of personal feeling. Here a nation in utter despair welcomed the one person upon whom it had fixed its hope of salvation. In this way did the House of Orange come back into its own—with a promise of a new and happier future—after the terrible days of foreign domination and national ruin.

Arrival of William I in Scheveningen

XXIV.

THE RESTORATION

Van Hogendorp did not witness this triumphal entry. He was sick and had to keep to his room. Thither the Prince drove at once, and together the old man and the young man had a prolonged conference.

What was to be the exact position of the Prince, and what form of government must be adopted by the country? On the road from Scheveningen the cry of "Long live the King!" had been occasionally heard. Was William to be a king or was he merely to continue the office of Stadholder which his fathers had held? Van Hogendorp's first plan to revive the old oligarchic republic had failed at once. The regents had played their rôle for all time. They had showed that they could not come back. They had lost those abilities which for several centuries had kept them at the head of affairs. The plan of Falck to create a government on the half and half principle—half regent, half Patriot—had not been a success, either. The Patriots as a party had been too directly responsible for the mistakes of the last twenty years to be longer popular as a ruling class. A new system must be found which could unite all the best elements of the entire country. Surely here was a difficult task to be performed.

The country to which Prince William was restored consisted at that moment of exactly two provinces. The army numbered 1,350 infantry and 200 cavalry. The available cash counted just a little under 300,000 guilders. The only thing that was plentiful was the national debt. To start a new nation and a new government upon such a slender basis was the agreeable task which awaited the Prince, and yet, after all, the solution of the problem proved to be more simple than had been expected. The old administrative machinery of the Napoleonic empire was bodily taken over into the new state and was continued under the command of the Prince. The higher French dignitaries disappeared and their places were taken by Hollanders trained in the Napoleonic school. The army of well-drilled lower officials was retained in its posts. Except for the fact that Dutch was once more made the official language, there was little change in the internal form of government. The modern edifice of state which had been constructed by Napoleon for the unwilling Hollanders was cleaned of all Frenchmen and all French influence, but the building itself was not touched, and after the original architect had moved out, the impoverished Dutch state continued to live in it with the utmost satisfaction.

But now came the question of the title and the position of the new head of the household. Was it possible to place the state, which for so many years had recognized an outlandish adventurer as its emperor, under the leadership of a mere Stadholder? Was it fair that the Prince of Orange should rule in his own country as a mere Stadholder where the country had just recognized a member of a foreign family as its legitimate king? The higher classes might have their doubts and might spend their days in clever academic disputations; the mass of the people, however, instinctively felt that the only right way out of the difficulty was to make the son of the last Stadholder the first king of the resurrected nation.

Before this popular demand, William, who himself in many ways was conservative, and might have preferred to return merely as Stadholder, had to give way. With much show of popular approbation he set to work to reorganize the country as its sovereign ruler and no longer as the subordinate executive of its parliament.

The first task of the sovereign, when on the 6th of December he took the government into his own hands, was to abolish the most unpopular of the old French taxes. The government monopoly of tobacco was at once suppressed and joyous clouds of smoke spread heavenward. The press was freed from the supervision of the police, under which it had so severely suffered. The law which confiscated the goods of political prisoners and which had been so greatly abused by the French authorities disappeared, to the general satisfaction of the former victims. The clergy, which for many years had received no salary at all and had been supported by public charity, saw itself reinstated in its old revenues. But the time had not yet come in which William could devote himself exclusively to internal problems. The question of the moment was the military one. The French still occupied many Dutch fortifications. They must first of all be driven out. For this purpose the three thousand odd men were not sufficient. But no further volunteers announced themselves.

The first two weeks of enthusiasm had been followed by the old apathy. Neither men nor money was forthcoming. Everything was once more left to an allwise Providence and to the allies. During eighteen years the people had paid taxes. Now they kept their money at home. For almost ten years their sons had been in the army. They were not going to send them to be slaughtered for yet another king. The allies might do the fighting if they liked. And it was impossible to get Dutch soldiers. Not until the old government had begun to enforce the former French law upon the conscription was it possible to lay the foundations of a national army. After a year 45,000 infantrymen and 5,000 cavalrymen were ready to join the allies. Then, however, they were no longer needed. Napoleon was drilling his hundred rustics on the Island of Elba, and the Congress of Vienna had started upon that round of dinners and gayeties which was to decide the future destinies of the European continent.

After the army came the question of a constitution. This problem was settled in the following way: A committee of fourteen members was appointed to make a constitution. These fourteen gentlemen represented all the old parties. A concept-constitution, drawn up by Van Hogendorp long before the revolution took place, was to be the basis for their discussions. On the 2nd of March this committee presented the sovereign with a constitution which made him practically autocratic. There was to be a sort of parliament of fifty-five members elected by the provincial estates. But except for the futile right of veto and the exceptional right of proposing an occasional bill, this parliament could exercise no control over the executive or the finances. This was exactly what most people wanted. They had had enough and to spare of popular government. They were quite willing to leave everything to an able king who would know best what was good for them.

On all sides the men of 1813 were surrounded by the ruins of the failures of their inexperienced political schemes. The most energetic leaders among them were dead or had been forced out of politics long ago. Of the younger generation all over Europe the best elements had been shot to pieces for the benefit of the Emperor Napoleon. The people that remained when this scourge left Europe were the less active ones, the less energetic ones, those who by nature were most fit to be humble subjects.

On the 29th of March six hundred of the most prominent men of the country were called together at Amsterdam to examine the new constitution and to express their opinion upon the document. Only four hundred and forty-eight appeared. They accepted the constitution between breakfast and luncheon. They did not care to go into details. Nobody cared. People wanted to be left in peace. Political housekeeping had been too much trouble. They went to board with their new king, gave him a million and a half a year, and told him to look after all details of the management, but under no circumstances to bother them. And the new king, whose nature at bottom was most autocratic, assumed this new duty with the greatest pleasure and prepared to show his subjects how well fitted he was for such a worthy task.

XXV.

WILLIAM I

On the 20th of July, 1814, Russia, Austria, and Prussia, together with England, agreed to recognize and support the new Kingdom of Holland and to add to the territory of the old republic the former Austrian possessions in Belgium. This meant the revival of a state which greatly resembled the old Burgundian Kingdom. The allies did not found this new country out of any sentimental love for the Dutch people. England wanted to have a sentinel in Europe against another French outbreak, and therefore the northern frontier of France must be guarded by a strong nation. To further strengthen this country England returned most of the colonies which during the last eighteen years had been captured by her fleet. But before the new kingdom could start upon its career General Bonaparte had tired of the monotony of his island principality and had started upon his well-known trip to Waterloo. The new Dutch army upon this occasion fought well and at Quatre Bras rendered valuable services.

General Bonaparte was dispatched to St. Helena, a fate which of late has inspired many sentimental folk to the point of writing books, and the Kingdom of Holland-Belgium could begin its independent existence in all seriousness. King William, in this new country, remained the absolute ruler. Instead of one there were to be two chambers in his new domains. But the executive and legislative power was all vested in the hands of his Majesty. He, on the whole, made use of them for the very best purposes.

In a material way he attempted every possible remedy for the poverty of the country. As far as dollars and cents go he was an excellent king. Canals were dug all over the country; commerce was encouraged in every possible way; the colonies were exploited with energy; factories were built with and without support of the state, and the mineral riches of Belgium were fully developed.

A plan for a Panama, or, rather, a Nicaraguan Canal was seriously discussed. And yet William failed. The task to which he had been called was an impossible one. Belgium and Holland had nothing in common but their mutual dislike of each other. Protestant Holland, proud of its history, had no sympathy for Catholic Belgium, where the Middle Ages had peacefully continued while the rest of the world had moved forward.

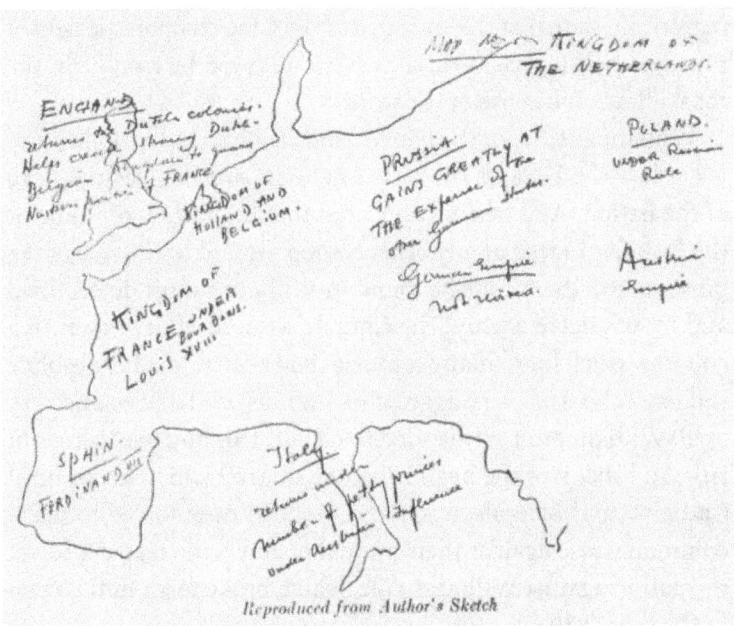

Reproduced from Author's Sketch

Kingdom of the Netherlands

Catholic Belgium returned these uncordial sentiments most heartily, and with the worst of prejudices awaited the things which must be inflicted upon it by a Protestant king.

A man of such pronounced views as King William was certain to have many and sincere enemies. Furthermore, the French part of Belgium, following the example of its esteemed neighbours, enjoyed a noisy opposition to the powers that were as a sort of inspiring political picnic. But the real difficulties of William's reign began when he got into a quarrel with the Catholic Church. This well-organized institution, which will provide all things to all men, under all conditions and circumstances, was directly responsible for the ultimate break between the two countries. We are not discussing the Church as an establishment for the propagation of a certain sort of religious ethics; but we must regretfully state that the entrance of the Church upon the field of practical politics has invariably been followed by trouble in the most all-around sense of the word.

William as King of the Netherlands felt his responsibility and felt it heavily. He and He Only (make it capitals) was the head of the nation. And when it appeared that the Bishop of Rome or the Bishop of Liège or any other bishop aspired to the rôle of the power above the throne he found in William a most determined and most sincere enemy. The Church, assured of her power in a country which for so many centuries had been under her absolute influence, became very aggressive, and her leaders became very bold. William promptly landed the boldest among the bishops in jail. And that was the beginning of a quarrel which lasted until Catholics and Liberals, water and fire, had been forced to make common cause against their mutual enemy and started a secret revolution against William's rule, which broke forth in the open in the year 1830.

The northern part of the country, for the first time in almost thirty years, began to take an interest in politics and commenced showing hopeful signs of life. And when in February, 1831, the commander of a small Dutch gunboat, Lieutenant van Speyck, blew his ship and all his sailors into the kingdom of brave men rather than surrender to the Belgian rabble which had climbed on board his disabled craft, such an unexpected enthusiasm broke loose that it took Holland just ten days in which to reconquer most of the rebellious provinces.

Lieutenant Van Speyck blows up his ship

This, however, was not to the liking of France. In the first place, France was under the influence of a strong Catholic reaction and felt compelled to help the suffering brethren in Belgium. In the second place, France did not like the idea of a sentinel of England and hastened to recognize and support the Prince of Saxe-Coburg, who was called upon to mount the newly founded throne of the independent state of Belgium.

A large French army marched north to oppose a further advance of the Hollanders. William had to give up all idea of reuniting the two countries. Since when, divorced from their incompatible companions, the two nations have gone their different ways in excellent friendship and have established great mutual respect and understanding.

To King William, however, who had devoted his time and strength quite as much to Belgium as to Holland, the separation came as a terrible blow. William was one of those sovereigns who take a cup of coffee and a bun at five in the morning and then set to work to do everything for everybody. He could not understand that mere devotion to duty was not sufficient to make all his subjects love him. Perhaps he had not always shown great tact in dealing with religious matters. But, then, look at his material results. The Prince, who seventeen years before had been hailed as the saviour of his country, now began to suffer under the undeserved slights of his discontented citizens and was made a subject for attacks which were wholly unwarranted. That the conditions in the kingdom were in many ways quite unsatisfactory, is true; but it was not so entirely the fault of the king as his contemporaries were so eager to believe. They themselves had at first given him too much power. They had without examination accepted a constitution which allowed their parliament no control over monetary matters. The result of this state of affairs had been a wholesale system of thefts and graft. The king knew nothing of this, could not have known it. There were private individuals who thought that they could prove it, but the ministers of state were not responsible to the parliament, and there was no legitimate way of bringing these unsound conditions to the attention of the sovereign.

And so the discontented elements started upon a campaign of calumny and of silent disapproval, until finally William, who strongly felt that he had done his duty to the best of his ability, became so thoroughly disgusted with the ingratitude of his subjects that he resigned in favour of his son, who, as William II, came to the throne in 1840. William then left the country and never returned.

What must we say of William II? We are not trying to write a detailed history of the Kingdom of the Netherlands. This little book merely tries to fill out the mysterious and unexplored space between the end of the old Dutch Republic and the modern kingdom.

King William II

Even these twenty years it does not try to describe too minutely, because on the whole (except for the people themselves) the period was so absolutely uninteresting to the outside world that we would not be warranted in asking the attention of the intelligent reader for more than a limited number of pages. William II was a good king in that he was a constitutional king. The year 1848 did not see the erection of barricades in the quiet Dutch cities. If the people, or, rather, the few liberals who had begun to develop out of the mass of indifferent material—if these gentlemen wanted another and a more liberal constitution very badly, they could have it as far as William II was concerned. And without revolution or undue noise the absolute kingdom which the men of 1813 had constructed to keep the men of 1795 in check was quietly changed into an absolutely constitutional monarchy after the British pattern, with responsible ministers and a parliament ruled by the different political parties. The budget now became a public institution, openly discussed every year by the whole people through their chosen representatives and their newspapers.

The king in this way became the hereditary president of a constitutional republic. There can be no doubt that the system was personally disagreeable to William II as well as to his son William III, who succeeded him in 1849. But neither of them for a moment thought of deviating from the narrow road which alone guaranteed safety to themselves and to their subjects. However much they may have liked or disliked certain individuals who as the result of a change in party had to be appointed to be ministers of the government, they never allowed their own personal feelings to interfere with the provisions of the constitution to which at their ascension to the throne they had sworn allegiance. This policy they continued with such excellent success that whatever strength the socialistic party or the other parties of economic discontent may at present be able to develop, those who would actually like to see the monarchy changed into a republic are so very rare and form such an insignificant part of the total population that a continuation of the present system seems assured for an indefinite length of time, which is saying a great deal in our day of democratic unrest.

As we write these final words a hundred years have gone by since the days of the French domination and of the many revolutionary upheavals; the nation of the year 1813, broken down under the hopeless feeling of failure, and the people, despairing of the future and indifferent to everything of the present which did not touch their bread and butter, have disappeared. One after the other they travelled the road to those open air cemeteries which they had so much detested as a revolutionary innovation, their ancestors all slept under their own church-pews, and their place was taken by younger blood.

But it was not until the year 1870 that we could notice a more hopeful attitude in the point of view of the Dutch nation. Then, at last, it recovered from the blows of the first twelve years of the century. Then it regained the courage of its own individual convictions and once more was ready to take up the burden of nationality. Once more the low countries aspired to that place among the nations to which their favourable geographical position, the thrift of their population, and the enterprise of their leading merchants so fully entitled them. The revival, when it came, was along all lines. Scholarship in many branches of learning compared very favourably with the best days of the old republic. The arts revived and brought back glimpses of the seventeenth century. Social legislation gave the country an honourable place among those states which earnestly endeavour to mitigate the disadvantages of our present capitalistic development and by direct interference of the legislature aim for a higher type of society in which the many shall not spend their lives in a daily drudgery for the benefit of the few.

The feeling that colonies were merely an agreeable asset to the merchants of the country and called for no special obligations upon their part gradually gave way to the modern view that the colonies are a trust which for many a year to come must stay in the hands of European men before they shall be able to render them to the natives for a rule of their own people. Finally that most awful and most despondent of all sentimental meditations, that "we have been a great country once," that "we have had our time," has begun to make place for the conviction that at this very moment no other nation of such a small area and insignificant number of people is capable of performing such valuable service in so many fields of human endeavour as is the modern Dutch nation.

The failure of the men of 1795, who dreamed their honest but ineffectual dream of a prosperous and united fatherland, the apparent failure of the first Dutch king who in the true belief of his own direct responsibility still belonged to a bygone age, have at last made place for a healthy and modern state capable of normal development.

Out of the ruins of the old divided republic—a selfish commercial body—there has risen, after a hundred years of experimenting and suffering, a new and honourable country—a single nation, not merely an indifferent confederacy of independent little sovereignties—a civic body managing its own household affairs without interference from abroad and without disastrous partisanship at home—a people who again dare to see visions beyond the direct interests of their daily bread, and who are given the fullest scope for the pursuit of prosperity and individual happiness under a government of their own choice and under the gracious leadership of her Majesty Queen Wilhelmina.

Brussels.
Christmas, 1914.

THE END

A COMPARISON OF THE FOUR CONSTITUTIONS OF HOLLAND

CONSTITUTION OF 1798

The Representative Assembly:
The highest power in the State, to which all other governmental bodies are responsible.
The Executive Council of five directors.
The Representative Assembly has the right of legislation, of making alliances and treaties, of declaring war, of discussing accepting the yearly budget, of appointing the directors of the Executive Council. It can grant pensions and has the right of pardon, and will decide in all such questions which are not explicitly provided for by the constitution.
The Executive Council must see to the strict execution of of all the laws of the Representative Assembly. It makes up a yearly budget which must be submitted to the Representative Assembly. It has the right to appoint diplomatic and consular representatives. It negotiates treaties and alliances, subject, however, to approval of the Representative body.
The Representative Assembly shall consist of one member for every 20,000 inhabitants. Every year the Representative body shall be divided into a second

CONSTITUTION OF 1801

A Council of State (Executive Council, in Dutch: Staatsbewind) consisting of twelve members.
A Legislative Assembly.
National Syndicate consisting of three judicial officers to control all officials of the State State and all departments of the government.
The Legislative Assembly discusses all laws proposed by the Council of State. It discusses and gives its final approval to all treaties (except certain articles of such treaties). It has to give its approval to any declaration of war. It discusses and approves the annual budget.
The Council of State (Staatsbewind) makes up the annual budget and proposes new laws to the Legislative Assembly. It sees to the execution of the laws which the Legislative body has accepted. It declares war (after it has obtained the approval of the Legislative Assembly). It is the highest power in all affairs of army and navy, and it has the right of appointment of the principal state officers. The
The Legislative Assembly consists of one single chamber of thirty-five members.
The members of the Legislative Assembly are for the first time to

chamber of thirty members and a first chamber containing all the others. (There were ninety-four members in all.) The Representative Assembly is to be elected in the following way: The country shall be divided into ninety-four districts of 20,000 people each. These districts are again divided into forty sub-districts (grondvergadering) of 500 people Stadholder, aristocracy, etc., each. Each subdistrict elects one candidate and one elector. If the same candidate was elected in twenty-one sub-districts he became a Representative. Otherwise forty electors choose a Representative from among the three candidates who had the largest number of votes.

Each year one third of the members of the Representative Assembly must resign, and a new election for their places must be held.

To be entitled to vote one must be either a Hollander who during the last two years has lived in the country or a foreigner who has resided in the republic during the last ten years. The voter must be able to read and write the Dutch language, and must have passed the age of twenty. To qualify as a voter one must swear a solemn oath to the effect that one abhors the Stadholder, anarchy, aristocracy, and federalism, and that one never shall vote for any person whose opinions upon these subjects are not entirely above suspicion.

The Executive Council is appointed by the Representative Assembly, but the members of the Council may not be members of the Executive. The first chamber proposes three candidates. The be appointed by the Council of State. Afterward their election will be regulated by law.

To be entitled to vote one must be either a Hollander who has lived in the country for one year or a foreigner who has lived in the country for six whole years. The declaration of abhorrence of the Stadholder, aristocracy, etc., is no longer insisted upon. A single promise to "remain faithful to the constitution" is now sufficient.

The Council of State is composed of twelve members. The first seven members are appointed by "the present Executive Council" (this meant the three authors of the constitution of the year 1810). These seven were to appoint their five colleagues. Each year one of the twelve members was supposed to resign. A vacancy was filled as follows: The departmental circles proposed four people. Out of those four the Legislative Assembly elected two. From among those two the Council of State then selected their new colleague.

The agents are replaced by small advisory councils of three members. They are responsible to the Council of State.

The Legislative Assembly meets twice a year: April 15 to June 1, and October 15 to December 15. The Council of State, however, can call together the Legislative Assembly as often as it pleases. The Council of State proposes all laws. Twelve members of the Legislative Assembly appointed by this body discuss the laws. The Legislative Assembly then accepts the law or vetoes it. No further discussion allowed in the Legislative Assembly.

The country is divided into eight departments. The provincial frontiers of the old republic are second chamber elects the member from among those three. Each year one new member of the Council is to be elected. After his resignation he is not reëligible until five years later.

The Executive Council appoints eight agents to act as heads of different departments (as ministers more or less). These agents are responsible and subordinate to the Council.

The Representative Assembly meets the whole year round. New laws are proposed in and discussed by the first chamber. Then they are submitted to the second chamber, which has the right of approval or veto, but not the right of discussion. The Executive Council must see to the execution of these laws.

The country is divided into eight departments with new names: The department of the Eems, of the Old Ysel, of the Rhine, of the Amstel, of Texel, of the Delf, of the Dommel, and of the Scheldt and Maas. Their former boundaries are given up and arbitrary boundaries are made. Each department is divided into seven circles and the circles are divided into communes.

Each department has a local governmental body somewhat resembling the old Provential Estates. Each circle is represented in this by one member. These seven members are elected by the voters. The officials of the commune are elected in the same way. These local, departmental, and civic bodies are responsible to the Executive Council.

reëstablished. Drenthe comes to Overysel and Brabant becomes the new, the eighth, department. Local government remains as before, but each city is allowed greater liberty in civic affairs, provided the city does not try to change the original idea of a democratic, representative government. The cities in this way regain a great deal of their old autonomy. The old interstate tariff scheme of the former republic is not allowed. But otherwise the cities regain most of their former power.

CONSTITUTION OF 1805

A Raadpensionaris.
A Legislative Assembly. (The old title of their High and Mightinesses is revived for the

CONSTITUTION OF 1806

A King.
A Legislative Assembly.
The King is assisted by a Council of State of thirteen

members of this body.)
The Raadpensionaris is
assisted by an advisory Council
of State of five to nine members,
to be selected by himself.
The powers of the Legislative
body remain the same.
The Raadpensionaris has all
the executive and legislative
power of the Council of State
(Staatsbewind) of 1801, but he
has at his disposal a secret
budget to be used "for the good
of the country" at his own
discretion.
The Legislative Assembly
consists of nineteen members:
Holland sends seven; Zeeland
sends one; Utrecht sends one; all
the other departments send two
members.
The first Legislative Assembly
is to be appointed by the
Raadpensionaris. Afterward the
departmental government proposes
four names. The Raadpensionaris
selects two out of the four and
returns the names to the
departmental government, which
then votes for one of those two.
Qualifications for franchise
remain the same as in 1801.
The Raadpensionaris is
appointed by the Legislative
Assembly for a period of five
years. The Constitution of 1805
lasted only for a year. The only
Raadpensionaris was
Schimmelpenninck.
The Raadpensionaris appoints
five secretaries of State and a
Council of Finance, consisting
of three advisory members.
The Legislative Assembly meets
twice a year for a period of six
weeks: April 15 to June 1, and
December 1 to January 15.
All laws are proposed by the
Raadpensionaris. The Legislative
Assembly does not have the right
of debate, but has the right of
members, to be appointed by
himself.
The Legislative body has the
same rights as in the year 1801.
The King has the same executive
power as the Raadpensionaris, but
may "upon certain occasions act
directly without consulting the
Legislative body at all."
The Legislative body consists of
thirty-eight members. Holland
appoints seventeen. The other
departments two or four; Drenth,
one. When a department increases
in territory the number of
representatives may be increased,
too.
For the first time nineteen new
members proposed by the
Legislative body itself and
confirmed by the King were added
to the old Legislative Assembly of
the year 1805.
The next year (1807) the King
appointed the new members from
among a list of candidates, half
of which list was proposed by the
Legislative Assembly, the other
half of which was made up by a
number of notabilities who were
selected by the King from a list
of names proposed by departmental
officers.
The Constitution refers the
question of the qualifications for
the franchise to the future. As a
matter of fact the franchise was
practically abolished after the
institution of the kingdom.
The King appoints four
secretaries of State (Ministers).
The Legislative body meets at
the pleasure of the King. It is
supposed to meet regularly during
two months of the year.
The King proposes the laws. The
Legislative Assembly has no right
of discussion. Can accept a law or
veto it.
The country is divided into nine
departments. Drenthe is revived as

veto. The same division of the country as before. The cities continue to regain their old sovereign rights.	a separate department. The old Departmental Estates, are brought immediately under the influence of the King, who appoints his own officers (Land-drost). The autonomy of the cities is again lost.

BIBLIOGRAPHY

GIVING THE DETAILS OF THE RESURRECTION OF HOLLAND IN 1812

For this period we have, as may be seen from the following list of books, very few memoirs, only a limited number of newspapers, and no books which show us in detail the inside work of the big and little political events of the day.

The rôle which the Batavian Republic played was so little flattering that the chief participants in the drama of national decadence preferred not to chronicle their own adventures between the years 1795 and 1815 and expose their private conduct to the public judgment of their children and grandchildren.

THE BATAVIAN REPUBLIC

Van der Aa, Biographisch woordenboek, the only source of information for the lives of many of the men of this period.

Appelius, J.H., de staatsomwenteling van 1795 in haren aard, loop en gevolgen beschouwd. Leiden, 1801.

D'Auzon de Boisminart W.P., Gedenkschriften, 1788-1840. The Hague, 1841-1843.

Bas, F. de, De overgave van de Bataafsche vloot in 1795. Utrecht, 1884.

Berkhey, J. le Francq van, de Bataafsche menschelykheid enz. Leiden, 1801.

Beynen, G.J.W. Koolemans, Het Terugtrekken van Daendels in 1799 uit de Zype naar de Schermer. Leiden, 1898.

Blok, P.J., Geschiedenis van het Nederlandsche volk. The new standard history in eight volumes. Translated into English. The part treating of the last hundred years of the Dutch Republic has not been translated as fully as the earlier history.

Bouwens, R.L., aan zyne committenten over het politiek en finantieel gedrag der ministers van het vorige bewind. Amsterdam, 1797.

Brauw, W.M. de, de Departmenten van Algemeen Bestuur in Nederland sedert de omwenteling van 1795. Utrecht, 1864.

Brougham, Henry Lord, Life and Times, written by himself. Edinburgh, 1871. This book contains a description of a voyage through the Batavian Republic in the year 1804.

Byleveld, H.J.J., de geschillen met Frankryk betreffende Vlissingen sedert 1795 tot 1806. The Hague, 1865.

Castlereagh, Memoirs and correspondence of Viscount Castlereagh, London, 1848, contains the diplomatic correspondence upon many subjects concerning the Batavian Republic and the Kingdom of Holland.

Colenbrander, Gedenkschriften der Algemeene Geschiedenis van Nederland. Collection of official documents. 1795-1798, 1798-1801 (2 vols.); 1801-1806 (2 vols.), 1806 1810 (2 vols.), 1810-1813 (3 vols.) The standard work of sources for this period.

Courant, de Bataafsche Binnenlandsche, a newspaper with some news but little of any value.

Covens C. Beknopte staatsbeschryving der Bataafsche Republiek. Amsterdam, 1800.

Dagverhaal der handelingen van de eerste en tweede nationale and constitueerende vergadering representeerende het Volk van Nederland. The Hague, 1796-1801. A sort of congressional record in twenty-two volumes.

Decreeten der Nationale Vergadering, March, 1796 to January, 1798. Twenty-three volumes. An enormous mass of state papers of the National Assembly.

Decreeten, Register der, van de Vergadering van het Provintiaal Bestuur van Holland. March 2, 1796 to January 31, 1798. The records of the provincial government of Holland, which succeeded the estates of Holland.

Doorninck, J. van, Het Alliantie tractaat met Frankryk van 16 Mei 1795. Deventer, 1852.

Galdi M. Quadro politico delle rivoluzioni delle Provincie Unite e della Republica Batava e dello stato attuale del regno di Olande. Milan, 1809.

Groen van Prinsterer. Handboek der Geschiedenis van Het Vaderland. Standard work written from point of view opposed to the French Revolution.

Hall, M.C. van, Rutger Jan Schimmelpenninck, voornamelyk als Bataafsch afgezant op het Vredescongres te Amiens in 1802. Amsterdam, 1847.

Hartog, J., De Joden in het eerste jaar der Bataafsche vryheid. Amsterdam, 1875. A discussion of the emancipation of the Jews in the Batavian Republic.

Herzeele P. van and J. Goldberg, Rapport der commissie tot het onderzoek naar den staat der finantien op 4 Januari, 1797. The Hague, 1797.

Hingman, J.H., Stukken betreffende het voorstel tot deportatie van Van de Spiegel, Bentinck, Rhoon en Repelaer, 1795-1798. Utrecht, 1888.

Jaarboeken der Bataafsche Republiek. Amsterdam 1795-1798. Thirteen volumes. A continuation of the old year books of the Dutch Republic. Minute record of official acts, documents, etc.

Kesman, J.H., Receuil van den zakelyken inhoud van alle sedert, 1795 gestelde orders van den lande, de armée betreffende. The Hague, 1805.

Kluit, W.P. Sautyn, Studies over de Nederlandsche journalistiek, 1795-1813. The Hague, 1876-1885. A discussion of the Gazette de Hollande, the "Nationaale en Bataafsche couranten," and the official newspaper of the State before the restoration of 1814.

Krayenhoff, Geschiedkundige beschouwing van den oorlog op het grondgebied der Bataafsche republiek in 1799. Nymwegen, 1832.

Langres, Lonbard de, Byzonderheden uit de tyden der onwenteling en betrekkingen van Nederland in 1798. The Hague, 1820.

Langres was French minister between 1798 and 1799. Nothing much of importance.

Legrand, L., La révolution française en Hollande; la République Batave. Paris, 1894.

Naber, J.A., Journal van het gepasseerede gedurende het verblyf der Nationale Trouppen in s'Gravenhage. January 21 to April 20, 1795. The Hague, 1895.

Notulen van het Staatsbewind der Bataafsche Republiek. October 17, 1801 to April 29, 1805. Twelve volumes of records of the proceedings of the Batavian Executive.

Paulus, Aanspraak by de opening van de vergadering der Nationale Vergadering. March 1, 1796. The Hague, 1796. A report of this speech is found in Wagenaar.

Rogge C., Tafereel van de geschiedenis der jongste omwenteling in de Vereenigde Nederlanden. Amsterdam, 1796.

Rogge C., Geschiedenis der staatsregeling voor het Bataafsche volk. Amsterdam, 1799.

Rogge C., Schaduwbeelden der leden van de Nationale Vergadering.

Schimmelpenninck, G., Rutger Jan Schimmelpenninck en eenige gebeurtenissen van zyn tyd. The Hague, 1845. See also under M.C. van Hall.

Staatsbesluiten der Bataafsche Republiek, April 29 to December 31, 1805. Three volumes of official decrees.

Staatscourant, Bataafsche. See Kluit.

Swildens, J.H., Godsdienstig Staatsboek. Amsterdam, 1803. Discussion of the revolution from an orthodox protestant point of view.

Vitringa, C.L., Staatkundige geschiedenis der Bataafsche Republiek. Arnhem, 1858-1864.

Vitringa, H.H., Advisen over de eenheid der Bataafsche Republiek, den godsdienst, de verandering der constitutie, de vermeniging der oude provincieele schulden, etc. Amsterdam, 1796.

Vonk L.C., Geschiedenis der landing van het Engelsch Russisch leger in Noord Holland. Haarlem, 1801.

Vreede, G.W., Bydragen tot de geschiedenis der omwenteling van 1795-1798. Amsterdam, 1847-1851.

Vreede G.W., Geschiedenis der diplomatie van de Bataafsche Republiek. Three volumes of diplomatic history of the Batavian Republic.

Vreede, P., Verantwoording. Leyden, 1798. Explanation of his official acts as member of the Executive.

Wagenaar. Vaderlandsche Historie. See the three volumes of Vervolg written by Loosjes and his forty-eight volumes of Vervolg which bring Wagenaar down to the year 1806. Stuart in 1821 wrote four more volumes which continue the Historie until the year 1810 is reached. The same tendency to endless reports of facts without any comment, except from the revolutionary point of view, is met in this Vervolg, which is only useful as a book of information.

For the pamphlets of this period see the last column of the Catalogue of Knuttel, Catalogus van de pamphletten verzameling berustende in de Koninklyke Bibliotheek. The Hague.

THE KINGDOM OF HOLLAND

Blik op Holland of schildery van dat Koninkryk in 1806. Amsterdam, 1807.

Bonaparte, L., Documents historiques et réflexions sur le gouvernement de la Hollande. Bruxelles, 1820. Translated into Dutch in the same year.

Cour, La de Hollande sous le règne de Louis Bonaparte. Paris, 1823.

Dykshoorn, J., Van de Landing der Engelschen in Zeeland. Vlissingen, 1809.

Fruin, R., Twee nieuwe bydragen tot de kennis van het tydvak van Koning Lodewyk. The Hague, 1888.

Geslachts—levens—en karakterschets van Louis Napoleon Bonaparte. Schiedam, 1806.

Hoek, S. van, Landing en inval der Engelschen in Zeeland, 1809. Haarlem, 1810.

Hortense de Beauharnais, Mémoires sur Madame la Duchesse de St. Leu, ex-reine de Hollande. London, 1832.

Hugenpoth d'Aerdt G.J.J.A., Notes historiques sur le règne de Louis Napoleon. The Hague, 1829.

Jorissen Th., Napoleon I et le Roi de Hollande, 1806-1813. The Hague, 1868.

Jorissen Th., De ondergang van het koninkryk Holland. Arnhem, 1871.

Jorissen Th., De commissie van 22 Juli 1810 te Parys.

Maaskamp. E., Reis door Holland in 1806. Amsterdam, 1806.

Rocqain F., Napoléon premier et le Roi Louis. Paris, 1875, with original documents.

Roel, W.F., Verslag van het verblyf des konings te Parys 1909-1910. Amsterdam, 1837.

Wichers L., De Regeering van Koning Lodewyk Napoleon, 1806-1810. Utrecht, 1892. The best book upon the subject which has as yet appeared.

See Colenbrander's Gedenkstukken, Blok, Groen, and Wagenaar.

FRENCH OCCUPATION

Bas, F. de and Snouckaert van Schauburg, Het 2de Hollandsche regiment Huzaren. Breda, 1892. Story of the adventures of the Eleventh Regiment French Hussars.

Daendels, Staat van Nederlandsch Oost Indie onder het bestuur van H.W. Daendels. The Hague, 1814.

The same subject treated by N. Engelhard. About Daendels, see his life by I. Mendels. For the colonial history of this period see also M.L. van Deventer. Het Nederlandsch Gezag over Java. The Hague, 1891.

Hogendorp D. van (brother of Gysbrecht Karel), Memoirs, 1761-1814. The Hague, 1887.

Hogendorp, Gysbrecht Karel van, Brieven en gedenkschriften. The Hague, 1762-1813.

Kanter J. de, de Franschen in Walcheren. Middelburg, 1814. Krayenhoff. Bydragen tot de vaderlandsche geschiedenis van de jaren, 1809 en 1810. Nymegen, 1831.

See Colenbrander's Gedenkstukken, Blok, Groen en Wagenaar.

THE RESTORATION

During the centenary celebration of the revival of the Dutch independence the events of the years 1812 and 1813 were made the subject of numerous publications large of volume and dreary of reading. The art of reproduction having been greatly perfected during those last years, every single scrap of document was dutifully copied and royal battles were fought about the exact wording of long-forgotten proclamations. Most of these works of history appeared in serials and many have not approached any further than the dreary works of 1814. In the second edition of this book it will perhaps be possible to give a complete bibliography for the years 1812-1815.

www.ingramcontent.com/pod-product-compliance
Lightning Source LLC
Chambersburg PA
CBHW020845160426
43192CB00007B/795